CLAIRE TR

QUEEN OF THE Bs
&
HOLLYWOOD FILM NOIR

BY
C.MCGIVERN

Reel Publishing

Copyright Carolyn McGivern © 2010

First published in 2012 by Reel Publishing
978-1-905764-17-4

Apart from any use permitted under UK copyright law, this publication may only be reproduced, stored, or transmitted, in any form, or by any means, with prior permission in writing of the publishers or, in the case of reprographic production, in accordance with the licenses issued by the Copyright Licensing Agency.

ISBN 978-1-905764-17-4

Carolyn McGivern has asserted her right under the Copyright, Designs and Patents Act, 1988, to be identified as the author of this work.

This book is sold subject to the condition that it shall not, by way of trade or otherwise, be lent, resold, hired out, or otherwise circulated without the publisher's prior consent in any form of binding or cover other than that in which it is published and without similar condition being imposed on the subsequent purchaser.

Printed and bound in the UK by 4edge Ltd, Hockley, Essex.

Contents

5	Introduction
15	The Early Years
66	At the Top
105	New Directions
132	Hollywood Means a Long Time Ago to Me
146	"Cut; Print"
150	Quotes
151	References
153	Awards
154	Filmography

The Claire Trevor Album

Introduction

Claire Trevor arrived in Hollywood after signing a contract with Warner Brothers in 1925 to work on a series of shorts. The film capital was at its most scintillating and experimental. She was both excited to be there and an especially exciting prospect for the star-makers. Young, petite, blonde, beautiful, talented, husky-voiced and with a theatrical background, she was soon in high demand by the myriad of rapidly evolving studios. Producers made more offers to Trevor than any other actress and she was constantly sought out by the top studios and leading directors.

Among her admirers were William H. Pine and William C. Thomas, also known as the 'Dollar Bills' because none of their films ever lost money and their interest gave an early indication of why her services were so regularly called upon. She was naturally gifted and quickly became a proven asset, the value of her image was pure business and she was made aware that her job was to be as professional as possible, to be part of a team whose product happened to be film. Unusually, because she came to Hollywood directly from her first love, the theatre, she already understood that movie-making was not an art form, but an industry that existed to generate wealth. Despite her youth she already possessed an honest, clear-cut, unglamorous view of the film capital. She had few stars in her eyes when she arrived as a girl living the 'American Dream', seeking success and willing to work long lackluster hours in order to create profit. Both personally and via her character constructions she closely reflected the dominant western ideology of the period.

By the 1950s the dream hadn't altered and when she was working at Twentieth Century Fox, Harry Brand, Publicity Director, told the Press, "You'd like Claire Trevor. She's strictly herself at all times and her pictures are amongst the best money makers on the Fox program. She has an Esquire figure. Her voice is low and throaty with a fascinating soft purring quality. She has the vitality of a shrew, the disposition of an angel and the looks of a queen. She is an actress with a capital A, but would rather be rated a first class painter. She is a pro in the best sense, loved by every member of cast and crew."

The versatile and prolific performer was a star who more than most represented the rapidly changing moods of her culture and time, moving easily along with her audience, between the high optimism and grandiose scale of Western frontier idealism to the forlorn desperation, depression, corruption and deep set shadows of Film Noir. She was unparalleled throughout her seven decade career which seemed to flow effortlessly, without fuss, tantrums or demands, from one movie to the next, from the long-running radio series she shared with Edward G Robinson to the stage and television. If Miss Trevor rested at all it was because she chose to, not because there was a lack of offers on her agent's desk.

She was the consummate actress of her generation, performing unerringly as the glamorous leading lady opposite every top male star from Robinson and Bogart to Tracy, Douglas and Wayne. Later, as the years rolled by, she made a seamless transition into flawless character actress, willing to tackle and give her all to any project that came her way.

Her career was also a paradox.

Whilst she generated profits for the studios, commanded respect and was held in genuine affection throughout the entertainment industry, she found personal reward and critical acclaim hard to come by. Performance came naturally to her and renowned director John Ford once told her that she was so good her effort would always be taken for granted, that only those in the know would understand the breath of life she blew into each role she played.

Perhaps, in the light of Ford's comments, it should come as no surprise that Trevor became relegated to mainly supporting roles in A pictures or more central roles in B movies. Nor that, despite being unexpectedly Oscar nominated as Best Supporting Actress for just a few seconds of powerful dialogue and a ninety second appearance in the movie *Dead End* (1937), or eventually winning an Oscar for her portrayal of a down and out gangster's moll in *Key Largo* (1948), she never really made it to the stratospheric heights of stardom that others of her generation took for granted.

There was always a static sequel to her most exciting jobs; fellow cast members invariably found that the very same pictures that were sure-fire spring boards to stardom for them, were quite the reverse for her. At the preview of *Dead End* the press came out raving about her and at that time it looked like she was on her way, but she returned to Fox from her loan out to Sam Goldwyn to be cast in the same corny action quickies which they had been putting her in at a rate of twelve a year. Meanwhile team mates including Humphrey Bogart, Joel McCrea and even the Dead End Kids raced to the top of recognition.

Sadly, it is perhaps also unsurprising that her body of work has to date largely been ignored by Hollywood historians. Invariably, the movies she starred in remain cult favorites and historically relevant, but her part in them goes almost unnoticed. Despite her magnificently sensitive portrayal as Dallas opposite John Wayne in Ford's *Stagecoach* (1939), a cursory glance in her direction might suggest she was subsequently type-cast in Poverty Row Westerns even as she later transformed into the bad-girl of

Film Noir. Wayne of course rocketed to stardom on the back of the film and, by rights, the same should have happened to her, but as he transformed into a leading light in high demand, she became unflatteringly known throughout the film industry as 'Queen of the B's', although also in high demand.

Movie makers knew that what they would get with Claire Trevor was a faultless performance, every time, so that, whilst she was most often associated with the numerous B movies in which she appeared, behind the scenes she was much more than a B movie actress, making some stunning appearances in major works that changed the face of American cinema history along with some classy reflections on the society she inhabited.

The diversity of roles she uncomplainingly attempted set her apart from her more demanding contemporaries and she remained the go-to darling of studio bosses seeking a thoroughly professional and unfussy actress. They were all well aware that for a modest salary she would almost single-handedly raise the level of what might otherwise have been a humdrum characterization into one of heart-wrenching clarity. The studios understood her true worth. She perhaps didn't, and by constantly undervaluing herself she became largely relegated from the top flight which was inhabited by Bette Davis, Marlene Dietrich, Joan Crawford and the like.

She also had frequent unlucky breaks. In 1945 RKO called Trevor to say they had a design for her stardom mapped out. They wanted her to star in *Murder, My Sweet*. The picture gave a shot in the arm to the career of singer Dick Powell and it made Edward Dymtryk's name as a director, but head of RKO, Charlie Koerner, died shortly after the movie's release, and Trevor's RKO career sank without a trace.

The offers never dried up, but she continued to be treated as an asset rather than a fully-fledged and competitive star. The pattern repeated itself when, in quick succession she made *The Velvet Touch, Corkscrew Alley* and *Key Largo*. Again Hollywood shouted that Trevor would be tops, only for her once more to be forgotten.

Whilst she may now be largely left behind in the rotting film vaults, she was an actress with a formidable force of will, talent and a determination to make good, one who in fact forged a unique and stellar filmography and was rewarded with three Academy Award nominations, winning Best Supporting Actress in 1948 and she also won an Emmy later in life for her role in *Dodsworth*.

Trevor inhabited a world of profound crisis and violence, her characterizations straddled a period of national achievement, but also a sense of bleak pessimism for the future. Her world was one full of national aggression, tension and conflict and her representations fluently drew on this as she moved from frontier heroine into Film Noir, pictures distinguished by a dim, shadowy appearance, dark overtones and unerringly filmed in black and white to suggest the dingy and foreboding reality, along with the sullen mood of fatalism of the era.

By 1946 critics were sensing the darker soul emerging in films produced in America, movies characterized by tone and mood rather than setting or conflict, they were also quick to notice Trevor's rare and undeniable gift for conveying mood. Now, more than any other major star, she came to represent the classic hard-boiled femme, finding herself the perfect fit in productions that roughly coincided with the war years and the early Cold War period; movies that reflected growing national pessimism along with a sense of corruption and hopelessness. In Raymond Chandler's words, "The streets are dark with something more than the night." Trevor's noire persona was right at home, cynical and disillusioned, she thrilled audiences world-wide and particularly in France where the genre was first officially recognized and named.

Film Noir offered portraits of complex female characters, unusually fundamental to plot development, which suited the subtle talents of Trevor down to the ground and gave her ample scope to grow. Here, she had the chance to exist as a champion alongside the biggest male stars of the day, where several distinct character roles suited her; she was offered the chance to be the innocent victim, caught up in circumstances beyond her control, there were the gutsy but sincere girls with a high capacity for love and finally there were the chances for the female who was willing to use her wiles to get her way, usually at the expense of the male counterpart. In what were often shocking performances, Trevor could portray the darkest sides of the female in a genre that was new, idealized and linked directly to the era they grew from. Her characters could be selfish, possessive, slovenly, calculating, callous and even masochistic, intelligent, shrewd and cunning, often lacking in morals, but always aware of her unique feminine tools. It was said that these movies made a lot of good women bad but few went bad as often or as well as Claire Trevor.

She had finally come into her own.

Only to find her career once again stalled. Oddly the actress who was so versatile, talented and willing to attempt anything, suddenly found herself type-cast and it was these performances that killed her chance of becoming a superstar more than any other single factor. As Tinsel Town's favorite moll, everyone knew, if you wanted a toughie, get Claire Trevor. She now became limited to second leads and shady ladies, the quintessential hard-bitten floozy.

Her acting gift could not be denied and her talent was possibly best summed up by Robert Wise who directed her in the film noir classic, *Born To Kill*, "Working with Claire Trevor was one of the best experiences I have had directing a female star. Claire was highly professional, very receptive to suggestions from the director to improve her performance. But also with a keen mind and instinct how to improve a scene. She was a fine actress and a lady of quality. Although she didn't attain the big 'star' name of some others in that period, she certainly deserved to be a big star from an acting standpoint."

Hedda Hopper, writing for the Chicago Sunday Tribune in 1948, commented, "In three specific pictures during the last several years Trevor has proved with performances and personality that she was entitled to be top of the heap in Hollywood. Claire Trevor has personality. People who meet her don't forget her. She stands with her shoulders square, her chin up, and looks directly at the person she is talking to. Her voice and manner of speaking have an unusual precision and the directness of a person who thinks clearly. A note of sincerity warms the low, throaty tones of her voice. But her experience, unlike most Cinderella stories, has been that there's nothing like a good picture to stalemate one's career."

When asked who was to blame for the repeated false starts, Trevor admitted it was largely her own fault and whilst many of her reverses might be unexplained, there had been plenty of occasions when she seemed to go out of her way to make mistakes. Because she had so many offers she had turned down plenty that perhaps with hindsight, she should have taken and she took others she should have left. She also may have followed poor advice. In 1948 she said, "Up until now I guess I've never known how to bang on desks or follow up on things. I suppose I really didn't feel the grand urge, because the old regime at 20th Century Fox had me appearing in so many pictures as a gal reporter covering three-alarm fires, and dashing in front of police cars and telling off the city editor.

"You had to work in those days from nine to six. And between the long hours on those dreary sound stages, the only satisfaction I could take in my work was that at least it enabled me to pay the family bills."

She worked harder than most in an industry that could grind anyone down. She was undoubtedly one of the most talented actresses of her era. She was liked, admired and respected. She worked with the best studios, the top producers and most revered directors. She was cast opposite the industry's leading men and more than held her own. She was never without work, and was still constantly sought out right up to her eighties. But there were also plenty of reasons she never hit the very top with any consistency, why she has been ignored by biographers, film students and historians, including the fact that she rarely presented herself to the public and very few people outside the industry really got to know her. Fans found it hard to identify her with their expectations of what a top movie celebrity should be. She had no interest in social life and was not a glamorous star seen all over town or in night clubs, "I give small dinner parties sometimes." If she was asked why, her reply was steadfastly, "I'm too busy or too tired."

She stubbornly refused to work on establishing herself a star image and she was rarely promoted in a concerted manner as a star by the studios. Instead she preferred to lead a private existence and was possibly too earth bound to become a mega-star of the Golden Era. She didn't act like a star in her daily life and she was rarely treated like one although her work was admired by the critics. She never had the slightest respect for the star system and admitted, "I didn't know that to make a career in Hollywood you had to become a personality."

And yet, Trevor's was unequivocally a success story anyway. Success gained the hard way ... and fully deserving of a modern retrospective investigating her relevance within her chosen field and within the society she inhabited. Fortunately, Claire Trevor provided much primary source material for the biographer in her generously in-depth oral histories. As far as possible, to maintain smooth flow in what follows, I have used her own words and referenced her many interviews separately.

The Early Years

Claire Wemlinger was born into a life of relative comfort on 8th March in Bensonhurst, New York. Sources disagree on the year of her arrival but in a 1992 Architectural Digest interview she confessed to being 83, "and I don't care who knows it." Which would mean she was born in 1909, although most sources suggest 1910.

She was the only child of successful Fifth Avenue custom tailor, Noel B Wemlinger, an immigrant Frenchman born in Paris and his Belfast born wife, Edith (Betty) Morrison. "My mother was born in Belfast and came to this country when she was ten." Her family lived modestly but comfortably, and artists, poets, musicians and writers abounded in her ancestry. Claire enjoyed a happy childhood, "I was an only child but had a wonderful time. I was about ten years old when I first worked on stage in *The Blue Bird*. I was in a chorus or whatever – I took several parts, danced across the stage and played one of several children. It was a professional production in New York. And I loved it. It was like a fantasy. I thought it was marvelous.

"But I liked being the leading lady best and later, I had to be princess or I went home."

Her father owned a custom tailoring business, "He did all the big important men who jumped out of windows during the Crash…that's where he lost all of his customers." He lost his business at the start of the Depression and the family moved to Larchmont in Westchester County, NY when Claire was a child and she attended high school in Mamaroneck New York. "Our house was within a block of the water and I was able to walk to school."

She continued to enjoy appearing in school plays but said, "It was just for fun." Rather than drama, her first real interests were drawing, painting and she was very athletic and enjoyed tennis, golf and swimming. She did admit however to going to the movies regularly with her mother and father and enjoying them, "I fell madly in love with Rudolph Valentino in *The Sheik*."

Her dreams of a college education were interrupted by her family's financial decline but at seventeen she started a short course at Columbia University where she became a member of Theta Beta Phi sorority. "I studied art and majored in conversational French. I was good at French. When my father and his brothers took me to lunch they'd only speak French and I wanted desperately to join in.

"I went to a lot of dances and parties, studied hard and just loved my life. I went to all the different proms at different colleges."

All her talent and ambition at that time was directed toward a career as an artist and she had no real interest in becoming an actress. She was focused, dedicated and attended all her art classes and was progressing well until a fellow student handed her an advertising folder about the American Academy of Dramatic Arts. Her life turned upside down when she instantly quit her classes at Columbia and enrolled at The American Academy of Dramatic Arts. She had gone along with her friend on impulse but enjoyed classes in diction and found it easy to remember lines.

Her family, like so many others, was suffering from the stock market crash. "I had to go out to earn something to help. I'd never forgotten *The Blue Bird*, and I began actively looking for stage work at the same time.

"I had learned how to fall gracefully, body motion, little exercises to get the walk and things like that."

She became excited by the stage and the chance to contribute financially. Her faith in the future wavered however when she was immediately given a student role that was way beyond her raw capabilities. She said, "I went along for the first six months. The second half is when you do all the Shakespearean plays. Instead of doing that I felt that if I got out and worked and got a job, I'd earn more, and that's what I did."

She never gave up on art and continued to enjoy painting all her life, explaining, "What you create with oils or water color is entirely, exclusively yours. It reflects you. When you paint, it's a challenge to the imagination, the aesthetic sense. Both are vitally necessary to the actor's equipment when he's creating a worthwhile performance. So to me, acting and painting are closely related. Painting is a wonderfully intimate thing. It gives you the opportunity to retreat from the world, to really be yourself without self-consciousness and this is a godsend to people of the stage and screen, who because of their work, are constantly 'on' all the time and find their time crowded with problems and demands, as well as with other people. You can get off by yourself, relax and recharge spent energy."

(After moving to Hollywood, she began studying drawing and painting with Keith Finch and Howard Warshaw, leading artists living in Los Angeles.)

Months later she met up with her college friend, Gregory Deane, who had had some theatrical success. Deane reignited her interest in the stage and introduced her to his agent. They were sold on her new career. She decided she may just as well have experience and she dreamed up a theatrical background. She created a fake list of credits and began hanging round casting offices. "I made up a brochure of what I had done on the stage. I pretended to be a New York actress and for every interview I gave the same line, you know, I was in this play and that and hoping nobody would catch me out."

Inevitably she did get caught out when one director told her, "That's odd, I put on that play, but I don't remember you."

She told no more lies as she toured the agent's offices.

"I had a very good friend, Martha Sleeper, an experienced actress who worked professionally. She was a cousin of this boy in Larchmont, John Murdock. His father was JJ Murdock who owned Pathe. Mr and Mrs Murdock were the richest people in Larchmont and Martha and I spent lots of time at their house. We had great parties. We all went to plays together too. Martha took me in her aunt's car to her agent's office. It was there we came up with the name."

The office junior finally found the name that was destined to go up in lights and she became Claire Trevor after flirting with the name Claire Sinclair. As they drove to the agency Trevor said, "There was a sign along the way – Sinclair Oil. I decided I'd call myself Claire Sinclair. Then I started using Claire St Claire. Later I was in the agent's office and a boy took a telephone book and put his finger randomly on a page and it was Trevor."

After many rebuffs she made it into stock productions. She was listed by agents as 5'3", blond hair, hazel eyes.

She signed with Warner Bros in 1925 after a scout put her in a series of Vitaphone shorts 1926-1930. "Those shorts only took a day or so to make."

On 30th December 1930 Trevor accepted a new contract offered to her by Warner Bros. Artists Bureau, the New York branch of the corporation. The new contract was signed on her behalf by her father who was bound to, "insofar as he is able, guarantee performance by Claire Trevor. The Father further authorizes and directs Artists Bureau to pay all compensation to said Claire Trevor."

Under the new contract, Warner Bros had sole and exclusive rights to their new artist for six months and she accepted that for $125 per week, she would only make motion pictures for them; with or without talking sequences, appear as a "legitimate" stage actress in its affiliated corporation's productions, and make any sound recordings for them. She would be paid one cent for the sale of every record, over and above her salary. She was not to make any public or private appearances, appear in any shows, make any recordings or engage in any other occupation without the written agreement of Artists Bureau. She was to pose, act and appear as ordered by the Bureau which also now owned her name for advertising, commercial or publicity purposes.

She had also, without any further payment, to be willing to work in authorized television and radio productions. She might work in stage and film productions simultaneously, and would, in that circumstance be paid double her agreed salary.

As with most studio contracts of the day, Warner Bros included a morality clause, and Mr Wemlinger agreed that his twenty one year old daughter would conduct herself "with due regard to public convention and morals, and agreed that she will not do or commit any act or thing that will tend to degrade her in society or bring her into public hatred, contempt, scorn or ridicule, or that will tend to shock, insult or offend the community or ridicule public morals or decency or prejudice the Artists Bureau or the motion picture industry in general." She was also not to commit any act that might injure her mentally or physically and must at all times conform to the terms and conditions of her contract.

She was to render her services in New York or Los Angeles but within the terms of the contract Warner Bros stated that Trevor would not be sent to Los Angeles until she had undertaken four months of stage training at the St Louis Stock Company, operated by Artists Bureau. Just in case Trevor did have to travel the contract stated, "Artists Bureau agrees to furnish Artist with two railroad and Pullman tickets to the Coast, and return"

The Bureau inserted a clause that it might lend, rent or lease Trevor's services to other producers and that in such circumstances she must work for them to the best of her ability.

At the end of the first six months, if her option was consecutively picked up, her salary would increase to $150 per week, then after the next six months to $200 and rising eventually to $400 per week.

Under the terms of her contract her stage debut was with Robert Henderson's Repertory Players in 1930 at the annual Theatre Festival in Ann Arbor. She was a member of the Greek chorus in *Antigone* and had a small role in *Lady Windermere's Fan*.

As part of her four months theatre training she then appeared in Summer stock on Long Island where she was the leading ingénue of the Hampton Players earning $5 a week plus a split of profits. Later she talked of "touring on a shoestring. We painted our own scenery and made our own costumes. We had one truck but labeled it 'Truck number 3'.

"We did four new plays every summer, which was quite ambitious. A new play is a big chore, lots of errors and rewrites. We all did everything. It was one of the best times of my life. Fabulous."

In an interview in Films in Review in 1983 Trevor said that the period provided her with the best training and reflected that modern actors don't get those same opportunities although admitted that stock actors tended to get stuck in a certain style of acting, in much the same way that television soap actors do today. "That was the theory, don't stay in it too long because you have to work too fast to digest and really delve into the meaning of everything. We didn't have time."

Trevor didn't always look back on those times so favorably and she admitted she lost a lot of weight, "It could be horrendous, physically draining, and mentally too."

Her first important appearance was playing Nina in Chekov's *The Seagull* in Ann Arbor, opposite Robert Henderson. "They had a brand new theater at Ann Arbor which looked very glamorous."

On returning to New York she made a series of shorts that were filmed in Warner's Flatbush studios.

In 1932 Alexander McKaig cast her in her Broadway debut, *Whistling in the Dark*. "Edward Arnold was in it, Ernest Truex was the star and they were wonderful. We rehearsed and opened out of town in a couple of theatres then came into New York. I knew it was a hit on opening night because the laughs were so full and often. We ran for nine months in New York when every play was closing in about two days. They asked me if I wanted to go on the road with it and of course I did. That's the first time I was away from my mother and father."

A New York critic enthused over her performance, "Miss Claire Trevor, a shiny debutante, plays the pretty heroine casually."

Eventually the comedy landed in Los Angeles where Trevor's performance was acclaimed in the LA Examiner, "In the cast are several types worth noting. Claire Trevor is delicious in her indifference."

Whilst she was there she was approached by several film companies offering screen tests. "I made tests at virtually every major studio. They offered five-year and seven-year contracts. I turned them all down. My heart was in the theatre. At MGM I made a test with Lionel Barrymore from a scene out of a picture. They used to take all afternoon when they made tests like that. It must have been a good test because Irving Thalberg said he wanted to see me. He said, 'Now why don't you want to join Miss Trevor? Why don't you want a seven year contract?' I said, 'Seven years is like an eternity. I want to work in theatre and maybe do a picture a year.' He said, 'Don't you know it takes seven years to make a star?'

She went for other tests but turned each of them down, preferring to return to New York, her focus keenly set on the theatre and Broadway, "Later, I paid dearly for the gesture. I didn't get another play for months. How stupid could you be? I think it was the biggest mistake of my life – not signing with Thalberg."

In part her refusal came because she felt she needed a rest and in part because she wanted another season on stage. Either way, during the difficult years of the Depression there was little theatre and Trevor was forced to do anything to earn some money, "I posed for Stetson hats at that time – I did a lot of modeling. Whatever came up I would do."

Whistling in the Dark had been a smash hit, but despite good reviews, her next effort, *The Party's Over* was less successful. "*The Party's Over* was not my choice of a play. I hated the part mainly because it was about an easy girl, a waitress in New Haven. I just didn't like the whole thing."

However, her own outstanding comedy appearance in the 1933 production resulted in further critical acclaim and she was offered a five year film contract with Fox Film Corporation. She accepted their offer saying, "This time I jumped. I snatched what I hoped would be the pick of the bunch – a 20th Century Fox contract." She and her father, who had agreed to her going to Hollywood as there was so little work available in theatre in New York, signed the contract on 5th May, 1933 and only on condition her mother went along with her as chaperone. Trevor said, "My father was so strict he insisted that my mother accompany me to Hollywood and live with me there. Well, she was ready for anything – she was full of Irish humor and love and excitement. She adored being on the set. When we had to work until two or three in the morning, she was thrilled – it was a party for her.

"I said to my mother, 'In six months we won't have to worry anymore.' You know they gave you these six month options then."

Two days after arriving in Los Angeles she was on location on a sandy wasteland alongside George O'Brien. "When I first went out I thought it was marvelous. I was treated very nicely, except for working too hard."

The Zane Grey western, *Life in the Raw* (1933), directed by Louis King, produced by Sol Wurtzel, was her first credited film role. Tenderfoot Trevor got O'Brien in trouble when he attempts to save her brother.

"Life in the raw was right. I was introduced to everyone at the studio on Western Avenue. I met the head of the studio and all the department heads, I was taken to the wardrobe department and fitted for clothes. I was told not to fall in love with my leading man. I thought, 'Are you kidding…George O'Brien?' Later of course I fell in love with him. I thought he was divine. He was so sweet to my mother and me and gave us good advice, took us to dinner.

"But doing the picture was so hard for me. First of all I didn't know anything about the technique of making movies. Making two shorts is not worth anything. I'd studied on the stage and that was what I knew something about. The calls were for five thirty in the morning which was the exact opposite from theatre hours. It was all so foreign and awkward and a western out on location all the time.

"Of course I didn't know how to ride a horse either. I'd only seen a horse in central Park. I had to learn how to ride. I was in almost every shot and we worked six days a week. We had Sunday off but worked on every Saturday night. It was hard, hard work."

In 1990 during a visit to the San Sebastian Film Festival celebrating the fiftieth anniversary of *Stagecoach,* sole survivor of the movie, eighty year old Trevor recalled the start of her career during the Great Depression.

She said that the title of her first movie became emblematic for what was to follow, "You had to be ready at five am to go out on location somewhere, you got made up in a bus, you were working until nine pm and sometimes later ... the conditions were shocking, yet in a way the units were like family, people did seem to be happy."

In quick succession through 1933 she shot another Western, *The Last Trail*, directed by Jas Tinling, again opposite O'Brien.

Reviewers of the picture made from yet another Zane Grey story weren't particularly warm but The LA Examiner briefly mentioned that Trevor was very pretty.

In a hurry came *The Mad Game* directed by Irving Cummings. Trevor worked here opposite Spencer Tracy and won excellent notices for her performance as a cigarette-rolling newspaper reporter, with Andre Senwald writing in the New York Times, "Claire Trevor is quietly effective" and Variety commenting, "She gave about the best portrayal of a newspaper gal which the studios have submitted."

She was full of respect for Tracy and said she immediately began to imitate the way "he throws a line away."

"I remember Spence being very, very impressed by me. This sounds braggadocio, but it was the truth. He said, 'This kid really has it.' He liked the way I delivered lines." She hinted that he asked her out several times, but said she turned him down because he was married.

From 1933 through 1938 Trevor starred in twenty nine films, often having either the lead role or the role of heroine and usually playing a sweet young woman in B movie potboilers and cheap westerns. Disillusionment swiftly crept up.

"I just did one picture on top of another. I made about six or seven a year and since I did all the leads that meant working, working, working. I played every kind of role. In one film I played a gangster's moll, in another I played a mother and I even did a musical. I didn't sing and they dubbed it while I mouthed it to the playback."

She was cast in an A film only twice in the period. In both *To Mary With Love* (1936) and *Second Honeymoon* (1937) she had parts that merely fed the stars but still she considered she was learning on the job and about delivering in hectic circumstances. She was playing a variety of parts, but found most success featuring as an American working girl striving to make her way. "I wanted parts that were believable. Instead I was often doing sort of crazy characters, the kinds of people I'd never met."

Even so her characterizations had enormous contemporary resonance and her working-girl heroines tended to be up-beat and determined, in keeping with the strong feminism of the era. She was seen as bright and free, capable of overcoming the hard economic times.

Photoplay suggested, "Claire Trevor is more than acceptable. The girl has personality and plenty of ability."

In 1933 she worked with director James Tinling on *Jimmy and Sally* playing a skillful secretary rising from her position in a meat-packing firm to head its publicity department, in love with the movie-lead, James Dunn.

By the end of the year Hollywood had already dubbed her "Queen of the Bs" and 1934 saw her starring in several more average Fox releases beginning with *Hold That Girl*, directed by Hamilton McFadden.

Once again playing opposite James Dunn, a witty detective, Trevor reprised the role of newspaper girl in *The Mad Game* (1933), becoming involved in one scrape after another in the comedy-adventure. As the wise-cracking reporter whose anxiety to find a headline leads her into the underworld, Trevor played heavy on the New Yorkese.

Jerry Hoffman wrote in LA Examiner Plays Film, "Simply because she played a girl reporter so well in *The Mad Game*, and does well in this, I do hope Claire Trevor isn't to be condemned to continual quarreling with a city editor. She seems to have something, but it will take varied roles to do her justice."

Wild Gold (1934) followed, directed by George Marshall and co-starring John Boles, Harry Green. Here Trevor played a nightclub singer in a modern rush to the gold fields abandoned by the '49ers. On this occasion she sang the soundtrack herself and the New York Times Review of July 24, 1934 commented "Claire Trevor's principal contribution is also the film's chief merit, namely, an attractive and pleasing song called 'If I Were Free to Fall in Love This Season.'

In the same year *Baby Take a Bow* (1934), directed by Harry Lachman and starring Shirley Temple and James Dunn saw Trevor play the mother of treacly Temple. The film took its title from the song "Baby, Take a Bow," which James Dunn and Shirley Temple sang in their earlier movie, *Stand Up and Cheer!*

This film was banned in Nazi Germany for its depiction of gangsterism and gun play.

She worked on *Elinor Norton*(1934), a movie directed by Hamilton McFadden and starring Gilbert Roland and Henrietta Crosman. A nitrate print of this film survives in the UCLA Film and Television Archives, but currently is not listed for preservation.

The screenplay came from a novel by Mary Roberts Rinehart about a woman who sets out to nurse her shell-shocked and mentally unstable husband back to a semblance of health. Her problems are complicated by the fact that the marriage had been a mistake from the start. Trevor plays the wife, in love with another man.

Muriel Babcock reviewed the picture in LA Examiner Plays Film, "Miss Trevor, bearing the brunt of a more difficult and serious characterization than is usually allotted to her blonde prettiness, does adequate although not brilliant work. It pained me however to see her, a woman who is suffering and unhappy, and far from the beauty aids of Hollywood and Paris, attain such a perfection of make-up and to acquire no lines of character. This is of course not her fault, but rather one of studio production."

1935 saw little change as she went through the motions again in her next movie, *Spring Tonic*, directed by Clyde Bruckman, starring Lew Ayres, ZaSu Pitts, Jack Haley. Here she played a bored rich girl escaping her dull fiancé on eve of their wedding to find adventure – supplied by circus performers, an escaped lion and a pair of moonshiners.

The film was often followed in the theatre by a vaudeville act, even when two pictures played on the same program. Leonard Maltin reviewed it, calling it a "dreadful screwball comedy; everything about this film is heavy-handed, even director Bruckman's reuse of gags he devised for Harold Lloyd and Buster Keaton in the silent era." It was based on the play The Man-Eating Tiger by Ben Hecht and Rose Caylor.

Muriel Babcock was less stern in her assessment in the LA Examiner 30th May 1935, "The film is lightly entertaining and with a few pleasant moments."

Occasionally Fox would offer her something a little less bleak and things looked up still further with her next performance in an excellent production, *Black Sheep* (1935) from Sol M Wurtzel, written and directed by the talented Allan Dwan and starring Edmund Lowe and Adrienne Ames. On a cruise ship a professional gambler, assisted by Trevor, comes to the aid of a young man victimized by a jewel thief. The young man turns out to be his son.

Louella Parsons wrote in the LA Examiner, "Here is a delightful picture with two stars much better known for their supporting roles. A young Claire Trevor is more lovely than I have ever seen her as the wisecracking girlfriend of Lowe. Edmund Lowe, a first line star during the silent era who never quite made it past supporting roles in the talkies, is a very believable gambler and Allan Dwan comes back into the film highlight with a bang. A simple little story just full of entertainment."

Also notable in the mid-thirties was the increased consistency surrounding the productions she now appeared in as she began working more frequently with Sol Wurtzel. They were together again for *Dante's Inferno* (1935), directed by Harry Lachman.

Again opposite Spencer Tracy, a side-show barker with a power complex, whose drive for success leads him into crime, Trevor plays his fretful wife. She later commented, "They tried to make this an A film – they spent a lot of money on it – but I thought it was poor.

"Rita Hayworth was in a couple of pictures with me and in *Dante's Inferno* she did a dance number with her father in the café. I think Fox signed her up then. She had real potential." (Hayworth's credit in the movie is as Rita Cansino.)

Trevor may not have rated the movie but The LA Examiner reviewer Jerry Hoffman thought it was a "magnificent production. This is Spencer's farewell to Fox. For Claire Trevor, it is the beginning of bigger and better roles. There is a definite magnetism in this girl, which needs proper developing. She has revealed in past performances a grand sense of humor and now reveals a feeling for tragedy."

However, not all the reviews were favorable with one calling it a 'hokey-pokey story' that was 'weak on cast' and the LA Reporter comments that whilst the picture is weak it's 'Spectacular treatment of Hell sequence' might save it.

Toward the end of 1935 she found herself again directed by Allan Dwan, this time in *Navy Wife* a movie based on the

Kathleen Norris novel, Beauty's Daughter. Here she worked alongside Ralph Bellany.

The picture was reviewed in LA Examiner as "An unusually good programmer starring a collection of good troupers such as Claire Trevor…who is particularly likeable and sincere."

Already cast as Queen of the Bs, being labeled a good trouper might have been considered a demotion.

The years were passing relentlessly without very much improvement in the quality of scripts on offer. Trevor was settling into the formulaic pictures that came her way but doing everything she could to raise the credibility of her own performance. In 1936 alone she starred in seven dull productions including, *My Marriage, The Song and Dance Man, Human Cargo, To Mary With Love, Star for a Night, 15 Maiden Lane,* and *Career Woman.*

In *My Marriage*, directed by George Archainbaud, she co-starred alongside Kent Taylor and Pauline Frederick. But *The Song and Dance Man* found her teamed once again with director Allan Dwan who she respected and enjoyed working with.

Trevor starred as half of a dance team in a story loosely taken from George M Cohan's play. When the movie first came out it was shown alongside the first version of *Three Godfathers* and Jerry Hoffman (who became something of a champion of Trevor) of the LA Examiner grumbled, "Either one of them is good enough to be a solo attraction. It wouldn't be fair to slight one and comment fully on the other. Each is unusually good. Tremendously big stars aren't present in their casts, which is why, I suppose, they are being double billed. It is particularly good to witness Claire Trevor doing something better than the sweetness and light ingénue. There is too much talent in the charming little blonde to be wasted. As the girl who comes up from vaudeville to musical comedy stardom, she shows some of the ability she's been compelled to suppress."

Her next film, *Human Cargo*, was instantly forgettable despite being directed by Dwan and co-starring upcoming Brian Donlevy, Alan Dinehart and again, Rita Hayworth, still billed as Rita Cansino. Trevor reprised her romancing reporter, but this time fighting smugglers.

In *To Mary With Love*, directed by John Cromwell and starring Warner Baxter and Myrna Loy, a higher than normal budget for Claire Trevor saw her with a lower billing. Parsons at the LA Examiner thought the picture warm and with a human quality that penetrates the heart. "A film saga about modern marriage." Trevor played 'the other woman' and Parsons felt she was a revelation saying this was the film where she turned into a fine, brilliant actress.

Brilliant or not made little difference when she was put in the unsuccessful *Star For a Night*, directed by Lewis Seiler. Trevor starred alongside Jane Darwell and Evelyn Venable in the story about the offspring of a blind European woman who writes her successful sounding letters from the US. When the mother comes to visit without warning, the charade continues as her children believe she would be ashamed of them if she knew the truth.

Next came *15 Maiden Lane* where Trevor was reunited once ore with Dwan and co-starred alongside Cesar Romero and Douglas Fowley. Trevor played an insurance investigator helping Romero trap a gang of jewel thieves.

Again directed by Lewis Seiler, in *Career Woman* (1936) she was a lawyer whose dedication and intelligence helped acquit a girl accused of murdering her father.

If nothing else, she was working steadily throughout the period, playing society belles, vamps and sweet young things, tough or merry, graceful or rugged. She was able to invest each persona with a sense of truth, partly engendered by her real life situation as a hard-working actress who had turned to stage and screen out of economic necessity.

Despite her early achievements and some critical acclaim, Fox didn't budge and continued to cast her in B movies and yet another string of them followed. The ambitious and talented actress was discouraged and longed to be offered more challenging roles, "I would have given anything to play the really marvelous roles that Bette Davis had."

Life was tough and uncomfortable for her at Fox. She, like many other female stars, found it excruciating to be out riding in the California sun in velvets and heavy costumes. None of the sound stages had air conditioning, "They had big fans to blow some air in but the stages would be red hot with the lights and especially if it was color because the lights they used for color were much more potent and radiated much more heat. And I didn't like locations much more. You'd be traipsing around in forests and hills."

All in all by the end of 1936 she was thoroughly disgruntled by life. She didn't care much for premiers either and she began avoiding them in the same way she stopped going to the "dailies", "I'd look at them and be ready to kill myself. I'd worry about this scene or that one… I was always disappointed. Instead of worrying about what I should be doing that day, I was worrying about what I had done yesterday."

Even though she did so little to promote her star image, she still believed she had earned a chance at something better and did anything she could think of to avoid the B pictures at Fox.

Every time another studio offered her something, she thought this was going to be her big break, "and then the parts were so insignificant it didn't make any difference."

She was reported being seen around town with a "handsome beau." Clay Andrews had been a friend of Trevor's from school days and she said, "Clay and I have been friends ever since I can remember. He used to carry my school books for me."

She refused to confirm any romantic rumors but in 1937 was hard at work on Fox's *Time Out For Romance*. Directed by Malcolm St Clair she co-starred opposite Michael Whalen, Joan Davis and Chick Chandler. Here Trevor is a runaway heiress who falls for nice guy Whalen after hitch-hiking a lift in his car. A jewel thief has planted his loot in the car.

In the same year she was loaned out to Paramount to work on *King of Gamblers*. "There I had the opportunity to meet Stravinsky. He knew the director, Robert Florey, who was French, very well. He came on set, had lunch with us and I had my photograph taken with him. That was the thrill of my life."

The movie starred Lloyd Nolan and Akim Tamiroff. Gambler murderer Tamiroff as Steve Kalkas, attempts to get reporter Nolan and night club singer Dixie Moore, played by Trevor, in his evil clutches. Kalkas sincerely loves Dixie and has arrived on the scene to hear her sing "I hate to Talk about Myself."

For Trevor *King of Gamblers* could have been yet another big break but still it didn't seem to awaken her own studio to the fact that she was now becoming recognized as a good actress and the LA Examiner reviewer commented that "She really deserves a better fate than B pictures, though there are plenty of people to argue that B pictures really play to larger audiences than the class productions, and that Claire has a big following in smaller towns. Maybe all our campaigning in Claire's behalf is unnecessary."

This same phenomenon applied equally to John Wayne, whose republic studio B pictures were adored all over America and were generating a huge wave of awareness. Both he and Trevor eventually reared the reward together.

But before Ford teamed the pair, perhaps the campaign should have continued because Fox soon had her back directed by Allan Dwan and playing another reporter in *One Mile From Heaven* (1937) a forgettable picture, despite its challenging story line of a black woman who is the mother of a white child.

She did however get another break when she was loaned to Samuel Goldwyn to work on a major picture directed by William Wyler. When Samuel Goldwyn had first seen the play *Dead End* about a gang of street urchins in New York he decided it was a piece of social documentary that everyone should get to see it. As a result he paid $165,000 for the play's idea alone. Lillian Hellman, one of America's best screen writers adapted it for the screen. The finished product cost him over one million dollars. Goldwyn said, "I consider it more than worthwhile because it may serve as more than mere entertainment. It may waken the world to the fact that unless we do something for our underprivileged children, we are permitting a warped generation to grow in our midst."

She co-starred alongside Humphrey Bogart and Joel McCrea in one of her most acclaimed roles and the picture that started her on the cinematic life of shame and, she and the reviewers hoped, would make Fox studio bosses and Hollywood, finally sit up and take notice.

"I'd done twenty films by then and I thought Wyler had called me because he had seen me in one of those, but during the interview he asked 'What have you done?'

'Do you mean you've never seen me on the screen?'

"He said 'No'

"I was interviewed for the part of the secretary which became Wendy Barrie's part. But on the way out of his office I asked 'Who's going to do Francey?'

"He said I'd be great for Francey and I said it was just a bit part. I wasn't used to that but I'd never been in a real A picture and I was thrilled to be in one with William Wyler who I thought was a wonderful director. There are many parts that are longer but you can't do anything with them.

"It only took a day and a half to film one of my shortest scenes with Humphrey Bogart and me. It was a very small part – just two pages."

Trevor was quick to acknowledge Wyler's contribution to her work, recalling that the director had told her to report to the set with her hair uncombed, "Wyler to me was pure gold. I loved working with him. Bear in mind I'd made some fast pictures with directors, some who were new and didn't really know what they were doing, and he was a real pro, and a genius and a man of taste. The night before I was supposed to shoot he said, 'you better come down to the studio about eight o'clock' but I had no wardrobe, so we went through the wardrobe department together. Down there you press a button and a string miles long comes out. Racks and racks of clothes that they gather through the years and he picked out a sleazy black satin dress. I put it on. He said, 'Yea I like that.' I had long hair then and he said, 'A hat, we'll get a hat', we looked at thousands of hats and then he said, 'I want you to wear stockings because I want them to have runs in them and high-heeled broken down shoes, an old purse and he said, 'when you go to bed tonight, get up in the morning and don't comb your hair. Come to the studio exactly as you get out of bed.' I wore no make-up except some lipstick. That was it. I felt dirty and run down and awful and it was marvelous. He had told me explicitly what he wanted. He gave me a wonderful feeling for the whole thing. I wished the scene had gone on forever. I could have worked with him for weeks. It only took a day and a half to shoot. I was so disappointed when we finished."

Wyler delivered a powerful adaptation of Sidney Kingsley's play, delving keenly into the social inequities of contemporary urban life and he successfully submerged Trevor's fresh blonde beauty into the characterization of an unkempt hardened prostitute and former sweetheart of gangster Bogart. Under his tutelage she delivered a powerful electrifying performance as a downtrodden streetwalker opposite Bogart that lit up the sensitivity of both actors.

The supporting role registered strongly with audiences and critics alike as the girl who had fallen on hard times. Her portrayal of Francey – just ninety seconds in the final cut, lit by cameraman Gregg Toland, where every second counted - was good enough to win Trevor a nomination for an Academy Award for the first time as best supporting actress. Alice Brady won it and Trevor was disappointed but also, finally, thrilled at what was clearly progress.

Whilst she was quick to credit Toland's lighting with her success and accolade, "Each cameraman could make you look like a different person depending on who lights you...very strange" she knew it had been her relationship with the director that had been special, "Wyler was marvelously meticulous and gave me explicit direction about where to turn my eyes, my head, not about the feeling or the mood of the scene. He was exacting in his technique but I appreciated that because I was still really the new kid on the block. He was an absolutely marvelous director."

She also enjoyed working alongside Bogart and McCrea. "Joel was so nice and so handsome. I remember hearing him on the telephone outside my dressing room, calling Frances Dee, his wife. He was talking to her in just the sweetest way and I thought that girl is so lucky."

She would go on to work with Bogart in several more movies and he became one of her closest friends. "I could never describe him to you because he was something special."

Reviews for both the movie and Trevor were first class with Louella Parsons writing, "My respect for Samuel Goldwyn as a producer has increased ten-fold since seeing *Dead End*. He has produced a powerful, human interest drama which could so easily have been unpleasant, but with the treatment afforded it, the drab, morbid drama becomes not only believable, but fascinating.

"Claire Trevor, on the screen in a much too short sequence, portrays a streetwalker. And how that girl troupes in that one scene. So effective is the performance that again we must commend Claire on her shrewdness and willingness to accept these small roles which give her the opportunity that bigger parts do not always offer."

However, despite the honors heaped on her after *Dead End*, producers at Fox didn't show Trevor any more respect than before and in fact thereafter only put her in their low budget material. Trevor said, "This kind of disappointed me. I thought maybe *now* I can get into A pictures, because *Dead End* was a very big picture. But Mr Zanuck never had faith in me. Why I don't know. Perhaps he may even have been justified. The point is that if he hadn't confidence in a player, said player might just as well up and leave at the outset. And that's what I did."

She said in 1983, "Today this could never happen. Today if someone's nominated for an Oscar, they make them a star right away. I think they push them too fast sometimes. But I was disappointed to have been in a very big picture with fabulous sets and then gone straight back to B pictures at Fox." She had hoped her performance for a rival producer would encourage Fox to regard her more highly but as time passed she began to be increasingly typecast as gangster's moll and a "take-charge" professional. She was earning larger salaries and some producers had begun to notice an unusually sensitive performer, but increasingly she felt she was on a treadmill going nowhere and her disappointment and frustration grew as, in rapid succession, she was placed first in a low-budget quickie, *Big Town Girl* which was directed by Alfred Werker where she played a showgirl, married to a thief, who runs away to become a singing sensation, and then, *Walking Down Broadway,* directed by Norman Foster.

In this Sol M Wurtzel production she co-starred alongside Lynn Bari in a movie about six showgirls and their respective fates with six boys. Reviews were not great with most concentrating on a divided interest that let the movie down and the lightly outlined characterizations.

She felt badly let down when her contractual employer made it so obvious that her talent wasn't rated. She began to doubt her own ability and now made little positive effort to win better parts at Fox although she admitted the studio did now give her a nice dressing room with a kitchen and living room as reward for the attention *Dead End* brought. Accommodation didn't rank highly on Trevor's radar and 1937 was a low point in her career, despite her Oscar nomination and increased presence.

For the first time she reviewed her career and even took a small break, taking time to relax and put some distance between her and the studio, "I went on only a few vacations in the thirties. I went to Palm Springs with my mother. We would stay at a ranch down there and didn't bother dressing up. It was blue jeans and boots."

She was still hoping that things would improve if she held out a little longer and as Fox threw her into yet another B movie,

Second Honeymoon, directed by Walter Lang, she found she enjoyed working with yet another Hollywood leading man, Tyrone Power. They started going out together, "He was a darling. I met his mother and it was getting serious. In those days we took dating much more slowly than now. I thought, 'If I get serious about him, I could fall in love with him in two seconds. But if I get serious, my heart's going to get broken because he's so handsome, he's going to be a big star and I'm going to be left crying."

Despite the split they always remained close friends and after he moved to Newport Beach late in his life he spent much of his time at Trevor's house.

Loretta Young played Power's ex-wife and Trevor, as Young's best friend, listens and advises.

Critic Louella Parsons again loved the picture, "Everyone is sure to be pleased. Claire Trevor as the blasé friend of the lovers, completes a really good cast."

Still Trevor finally realized there was little left to hope for except crumbs at Fox and, greatly discouraged, she accepted an offer of a radio career. Her friends had all been trying to persuade her it would be a good move, but she had held out against them as she waited for Fox to come good. "I never do anything but what feels best in my own mind. It's still the only way I know to get what I want."

She hadn't got what she wanted and now she began a three year run in the CBS radio series *Big Town*, co-starring with Edward G Robinson as his girl Friday, Lorelei. The move doubled her contracted salary by over $1000 a week and made her twice as famous as before.

She also found she enjoyed working on radio, "Besides that, I was on almost every radio show you can name. I adored radio. It was heaven because you didn't have to be photographed and you had an audience. You didn't have to memorize anything, you just read it. Radio was my favorite medium."

Big Town was about a newspaper called The Illustrated Press and Edward G Robinson was the editor, Steve Wilson. Lorelei was the society editor, "In the beginning each actor had a wonderful characterization. Robinson would be playing the piano and talking about music and it had real depth. Irving Caesar wrote that. But later Robinson took over and gobbled up the whole show. It got to be a joke in the radio industry that he'd say, "Wait for me in the car, Lorelei." He'd go in and play his big scene then come back to the car. I'd say, 'What happened Steve?' And he'd tell me. It became a soapbox in which Robinson got on and spouted forth all his views. When it got more and more into politics, it turned me off. I was never into organization or movement…was never that kind of person."

The series was produced by Clark Andrews, a big, handsome radio writer and romance was quickly in the air.

Andrews was shy and at first Trevor had no idea that this was her new boss until he called at her home three days after she had accepted the role, to sign her contract and go over scripts with her. As they settled to reading the script Trevor was astounded to find Andrews was far from the typical Hollywood big shot. He was well educated and came from a wealthy background, he'd even studied at the Sorbonne. He was a gentleman that Trevor found herself instantly attracted to. "A movie actress simply doesn't meet young, sincere, unspoiled men." She was swept off her feet and into a whirlwind romance.

She had always found her co-stars and leading men too adept at turning their charm on and off. In California she had found it hard to meet men saying, "Movie studios glamorize you and pay you more money than you could ever earn anywhere else, but their shooting plans frequently go haywire and you are liable to be still in front of the cameras when others are out enjoying carefree fun."

She felt she could trust Andrews and the relationship deepened. Because they worked together she was able to give him more time than she had been able to spend with any other man.

Trevor and Andrews adored each other immediately. They settled in New York and in 1938 Trevor confirmed she would marry the Yale graduate who enjoyed playing tennis with her. Andrews went on to become a writer at 20th Century Fox. Trevor handed her Los Angeles mansion over to her parents and began living life as a housewife, dependent on Andrews.

"Before I married I depended on my mother for everything. I'm the forgetful type. She did all my remembering for me. I used to say 'when I marry it will be to someone who can take care of everything for me' ... so I married someone even more forgetful than I am. Then I became the efficient type, which proves a theory ... men never change. You might as well realize that when you marry a man."

Luxury for the newlyweds was going to bed early with books and candy, "I love candy in bed." They would read till midnight then, "I'd bring up some more food and the nightly ice-box raid began."

They may have eaten all through the night together, but Claire obstinately refused to breakfast with her husband, stating, "I will never have breakfast with Clark – I don't believe in a husband and wife having breakfast together."

Although *Big Town* proved a huge hit, Trevor quit after three years because Robinson, who had script control, began cutting her part to boost his own. "My part was getting smaller and smaller. My contract called for a raise but they wanted me to go on for the same money. Robinson was due a raise and he wouldn't go on without it. I said, 'Why should I go on for the same amount when Robinson won't? You can have your show.' She left, but said later, "I was in a butcher shop and asked how much the lamb chops were. Before the butcher looked up he said, 'Lorelei Kilbourne!' I thought, 'My god, the show had impact, I shouldn't have left it.

"My relations with Robinson were never unfriendly and we worked on several pictures together. He had great technique and such an expressive face."

Until 1938 she had retained her contract at Twentieth Century Fox but had never seen eye to eye with studio boss Darryl F Zanuck, "I wasn't his type at all. He liked the musical stars and the real glamour girls and I don't think he ever thought of me for any picture. He wasn't making the kind of pictures I could do."

Once her contract expired, although the studio said it wanted her to sign a new one, she felt it was now more than time to move on. She chose to return to Warner Bros. as a freelancer and immediately found herself working on a major production, again sharing credits alongside Edward G Robinson.

Trevor was taking a gamble by not signing up for any fixed assignments but Warner executive producer Hal B Wallis signaled his interest in her by notifying Fox of his intentions to pick her up, ensuring there would be no later conflict of interest between the two studios. Trevor was out of contract but sheltered under the wing of one of Hollywood's leading producers, one who seemed genuinely keen to work with her.

She had undoubtedly been Wallis's first choice for the part of Jo Keller in his upcoming movie, *The Amazing Doctor Clitterhouse* (1938), a gangster comedy starring Robinson and her old friend, Humphrey Bogart, with Trevor again playing a woman of dubious morals. Hal Wallis signed off her test, wardrobe and hair changes personally.

The Amazing Doctor Clitterhouse (1938) was adapted and scripted by John Huston and John Wexley from the hit Barre Lyndon stage play, and was directed and produced by Anatole Litvak.

Trevor starred as a glamorous gang leader masterminding robberies of expensive furs in a role that was trenchant in its criticism of society.

Furs valued at $200,000 were transported to Warner Bros studios in an armored car for the scenes where the gang robs a furriers. One chinchilla wrap was valued at $50,000. Each fur was heavily insured by insurance companies which provided armed guards to ensure that none disappeared during scenes. At the end of each day's shooting the furs were loaded into an armored truck and taken back to storage.

Trevors' costumes were designed by Milo Anderson who said, "A woman's clothes tell the story of what she is or wants to be." In the beginning of the picture she is illustrated as a product of the slums, a consort of thieves and gamblers, and when she first meets the suave doctor she is badly overdressed. She immediately understands that he isn't like the other men she knows and becomes acutely conscious of the difference in their backgrounds. She makes a pathetic attempt to appear glamorous in more formal gowns. Once she realizes she isn't attracting his attention she suddenly becomes ultra conservative and Anderson dresses her in chic, simple ensembles for the rest of the picture.

Her tests had eventually been rushed through by Wallis following a delay due to a bout of sickness but she was ready for action on Stage 4 at 1pm on 5th March. Her contracted salary was $2500 per week with a four week guarantee.

Whilst Trevor had been the first choice of Wallis, much haggling had gone on amongst studio and casting heads over the male stars. Associated Producer, Robert Lord argued with leading executive, Wallis, favoring Charles Boyer for the part of Dr Clitterhouse and sending a memo suggesting that, "The contrast between a distinguished Frenchman and the gangsters would be funny…

"I don't see that changing the name Clitterhouse to Reynard would be too serious. After all the play was only a London success…the title Clitterhouse means practically nothing."

Lord also briefly considered Cary Grant but added, "He is good looking, pleasing and personable, but confidentially, he is not an educated gentleman; and for that reason would not be quite as convincing in the part as Boyer."

The story is based entirely on the contrast between a handsome, suave physician and the low, cheap thieves he is forced to become associated with. When the name Edward G Robinson was thrown into the pot, Lord became enraged, "Eddie is the direct opposite of handsome and suave. Put him with a gang of thieves as their leader and, to our audience, it will appear as if he is fulfilling his natural destiny…Eddie as the doctor would reverse all our values and, I believe, sadly puzzle an audience.

"Let us reconsider this matter and refrain from rushing into a commitment which may destroy a valuable piece of property."

As it turned out Lord's opinion was over-ruled and he was still paying the price as the movie was on the threshold of release and on July 14th 1938 he wrote to Wallis, "Your friend Mr

Robinson just called me and asked to make a retake on Clitterhouse. Some of his friends told him that something was a little wrong about his characterization!"

He ended the letter drily, "Aren't actors wonderful?"

In fact Robinson had been to see the play in London several times and had making pointed hints to Warner Bros for some time before he was finally selected for the part.

Long before the cameras rolled the proposed picture had come under the scrutiny of film censor, Joseph I Breen and Warner Bros had already been advised that the picture was not acceptable under the Production Code when Breen told Jack Warner that it had not been clearly established that a criminal and murderer was properly punished by "due process of law, and the question of right and wrong was left in doubt."

He went on that "scenes showing the commission of crimes…would probably be subjected to severe mutilation on the part of political censor boards."

He further noted that the British Censor Board would view unfavorably any material suggesting insane characters in a motion picture. Wallis went ahead anyway, deciding to argue with Breen later.

In turn he also began to doubt his choice of star, passing frequent comment about scenes centering on Robinson, "If he doesn't sound like a nonce in it, and act like it, it is the next thing to it." As production continued he admitted Robinson's performance had picked up but warns Litvak, "Don't let him get away with any of his stuff and watch him closely."

Of course Trevor and Robinson had already worked together closely on the *Big Town* radio show and much of the marketing for the movie revolved around the pair, advertising,

"The year's most popular star-team...Millions are ready to see them on the screen at last."

Regarding Trevor, Wallis told Litvak, "In the scene where she slaps Robinson in the face, have her really let it go – not one of those dainty little taps with her fingertips." A little production revenge?

Trevor and the rest of the cast had their own problems with the director however, who was frequently late arriving on set, and Jack Warner took the side of the stars admonishing him for keeping "the entire crew waiting. This does not make good arithmetic Anatole."

To while away some of the tedious moments Trevor started a game of "What I would soonest not do," on set amongst fellow stars, with, "I would sooner not wear such high heels." The three and a half inch shoes had been giving her backache and between scenes she wore slippers and taught co-stars to knit. Robinson soon joined in with "I would sooner not play a role where I can't smoke a cigar." In *Clitterhouse* he had been limited to one cigarette in one scene. Bogart came up with, "I would sooner not get bumped off in every picture I make."

By the time the movie opened, the publicity machine was working flat out and Trevor found herself at the center of it all. Warner Bros spared no expense promoting her and the treatment more than made up for the old Fox days and at last she felt valued as a film star.

Trevor said of the PR machine, "It's nice to be naughty." She said it had been fun to play a receiver of stolen property, "I liked Jo Keller a lot. She has a real personality. Nothing lah-de-da about her and she proves she can step out in a tough racket and hold her own with the gangsters.

She had been on an uphill struggle for three years despite winning plenty of critical acclaim. Even her smallest roles she all but dwarfed the bigger stars. She liked to play characters, parts she could get her teeth into, "Not necessarily good characters either. Something more than just milk and water." At this stage of her career she could afford to state that she was sick of the heroines who never did anything wrong, "It does me good to kick over the traces once in a while."

The Amazing Dr Clitterhouse was billed as a bizarre, exciting and amusing story, in which Robinson gave his greatest performance as a highly respected neurological surgeon whose interest in the mental and physical reactions of criminals at the moment they were engaged in illegal activities becomes an obsession. Eventually he decides to use himself as a guinea pig and he embarks on a career of ruthless crime.

Clitterhouse meets 'fence' Jo Keller and he is soon the leader of the gang formerly led by Bogart. Eventually the doctor murders his rival and has to stand trial, one of the high spots of the movie.

For the role Robinson haunted hospitals and clinics and took lessons on how to play a neurosurgeon.

To date *Clitterhouse* gave Trevor her best opportunity and the critics who saw the preview predicted the role would elevate her to stardom.

In national reviews all the cast were praised. *The Indianapolis Times* praising Trevor's adept performance of a meaty role. *The Chicago American* suggested that Trevor had acquired new honors (and a new hair-dress) as the fence dedicated to crime because she thinks it more honest than big business and *The Chicago Times* loved the "deft performance of an actress we like."

More hard-boiled *Picture* however was less than impressed, "The plot seems excellent movie material on the surface, but the screenplay by John Wexley and John Huston as directed by Litvak lacks decisiveness. If it was intended as high satire, it is too high for average comprehension. If the intent was serious, the comedy elements are over-stressed." The critic did however add, "Miss Trevor delivers a well-considered characterization."

It seemed she had played the role exactly as she should and her effort was quietly applauded by the critics, of course most of the reviews concentrated on Robinson. She was billed just below Robinson on all publicity material and on the film credits but was clearly one of the also-rans when it came to the reviews.

After the picture completed Trevor and Andrews moved back to Hollywood where they rented a small house. But she continued to refuse a long-term contract with Warner Bros, or any other studio, saying , "I didn't want that so I sort of free-lanced. I made pictures everywhere ... Universal, Paramount, RKO, Columbia and Metro.

"I think Metro was the finest, although Sam Goldwyn Studio had the reputation of doing everything with absolute perfection, real style and class...but Metro knew how to build stars I think better than any other studio. It seems that most other studios got stars by accident and kept them alive but Metro really nurtured people and built them."

Warner Bros had wanted her to sign up for a five year stint, telling her they wanted her to be their "Oomph Girl." Although she turned them down, once more she later regretted it saying that Warners did make the kind of movies that suited her talents. "I was foolish and Ann Sheridan became the "Oomph Girl" instead."

Still her next picture, *Valley of the Giants* (1938) was a Warner Bros release and her first Technicolor picture for the studio. She was also seen for the first time as a loose lady in Western surroundings. She said in an interview in Classic Images in 1998, "It was a lovely experience, shot in Eureka, California, where the giant redwoods are. We drove out to the location every day." She recalled the men enjoyed the location work more than she did saying they all acted like big strong outdoor types.

Valley of the Giants was directed by William Keighley and starred Wayne Morris and Charles Bickford. It was produced by Lou Edelman.

Lumberjack Morris fights to protect the California redwood forests. In 1952 the picture was re-made as *The Big Trees* and starred Kirk Douglas.

Nitrate and safety prints of this film survive in the UCLA Film and Television Archives.

The weather on location was so bad during April and May 1938 around Eureka that many of the exterior shooting days had to be postponed, the director was forced to send a memo to Jack Warner, "I hope you will understand when I tell you that it is raining so bad that we cannot shoot. We expect this to be a hard location, so please bear with us and know that we are doing the best we can for your interests."

Not only had the director been hit by the elements he had never been overly impressed with the scripts and had raised several concerns with producers, particularly about the love story between Morris and Trevor, "One reason it was so difficult for the writer of the first drafts to get a love scene is that his girl has to fight for a hundred and seventy pages to cure the first vivid impression we get of her, namely, that she is a dance hall prostitute. Her introduction is extremely unsympathetic. She is a crook and a companion of crooks. The fact she has a Heart of Gold is no excuse." As far as he was concerned things had to change. "I'll grant you that something has to clean her up, but I can't somehow swallow a redwood tree."

In fact several re-writes about the relationship between Morris and Trevor were created before Warner refused to consider any further expensive alterations. Keighley had continued to anger the producers by cutting scenes and adding others. Producer Lou Edelman sent a memo to Hal B Wallis, "Everyone who worked on the script worked very hard getting it together, I think he should shoot it as it was written, and if anything is so obviously bad that it needs rewriting, I think it should be discussed first."

Wallis was more concerned with inefficient shooting and told Keighley, "Fifteen takes in Technicolor is more than yours and my salaries in a week, and if everybody doesn't understands this by now, we had better let them know about it. There's no reason for fifteen takes. And if you run into trouble again with the talent let's stop where we are and go into a close-up."

With rescheduled endings for the picture written Trevor was notified of two extra days of shooting. Although Keighley never had any cause for complaint of his female lead he did memo Jack Warner about the inability of Wayne Morris to learn his lines which he said had also held production up, "Mr Morris is causing us a great deal of delay. I don't think the boy is taking his work seriously, at least, he is not trying very hard. I am disgusted with him. If he could learn his lines and get some 'guts' in his work we could save a lot of money on our budget."

Wallis became increasingly fraught and next turned his attention to Trevor, telling Keighley, "Claire Trevor's first outfit, with the butterflies is out. Throw out the whole costume. Her second outfit is OK. Outfit number six; I don't like the light blue. It is entirely out of place and out of keeping with the sequence. If we can use it elsewhere in the picture, fine, but not at this point. Don't have her so dressed up. Let her begin wearing more western costumes. Put her in flannel shirts by this time in the story. I don't want to see her in fussy, frilly, typically eastern things."

He wasn't altogether happy about the color either, "Morrell has a peculiar thinnish spot of hair on the right side just at the hairline. Look at this and see what can be done. The Technicolor tests came back and when Claire Trevor wears any of the low-cut evening gowns, be sure that she has body make-up on her chest, arms and shoulders." In later tests he said, "I still don't like her make-up. It looked blotchy and dirty. I know this can be improved."

Producer Edelman wrote back to Wallis, "They are trying to overcome bad skin. She has blotches over her face and they are experimenting in an attempt to correct it. The Make-up department are doing everything they can to improve it."

Wallis was also unhappy about her hair, "As quickly as we can, make further hairdress tests. I didn't like the last test." He added, "All of her wardrobe is to be tested in COLOR before the picture starts."

Trevor herself later added, "I think they probably touched the color up. I don't remember having red hair, but I had red hair in this picture. When we shot indoors the lights were twice as strong as normal and very hot. I think color was worth it but I think many dramas are better in black and white. They have a mood about them that you don't get in color. When they first started, the color was so vivid. It's better now. I hate colorization. It's destroyed a lot of good films."

Warner Bros legal team ensured Trevor had equal top billing with Morris and stated, "She must have first female billing on main title and in all paid publicity and advertising, "Only the name of Wayne Morris may precede hers." Her contract was for $2500 per week and for a minimum of four weeks.

Her career seemed to be on the up at long last, although in 1938 she did another black and white movie for Twentieth Century Fox. In *Five of a Kind* she appeared as reporter Christine Nelson in a movie based on the celebrity Canadian Dionne quintuplets. This was their third film and, now aged four, they sang, danced and played with puppies. The movie was considered to be charming and was well liked by the critics even if it wasn't a major A picture. At least such Fox pictures maintained high production standards and were usually a grade above the standard fare for other studios and definitely above those produced by the many independents that were springing up throughout Hollywood. Trevor never did appear in any cheap or shoddy material.

In *Five of a Kind* Trevor's performance was, as usual, highly rated and her intuitive grasp of characters had now brought her to the attention of John Ford who was busy trying to cast a new film he was preparing to direct and produce.

Ford was at the top of his game and there wasn't an actor who wouldn't jump at the chance to work with him, but *Stagecoach* would prove to be special for everyone concerned even though the story had already been turned down by the big studios. Trevor was fortunate that when Ford came knocking she wasn't under contract and was free to take a risk with Walter Wanger Productions, one of the independent companies.

Wanger had actively informed the world that "This is Ford's picture," but it was recognized that without him the stand out picture would never have been made at all. The major companies had turned down the chance to make what they saw as a static Western where much of the exploration of the struggle between law and order, chaos and intolerance happens on a hazardous stagecoach trip to Lordsburg with an oddly assorted ensemble of misfits.

Each of the passengers has his or her individual problem. A child is born, there is an escaped prisoner out to avenge to murder of his brother, a dance-hall beauty, a fine, eastern lady, a gambler, an alcoholic doctor and a whiskey salesman. Unexpected alliances are forged and courage and integrity rise and fall in unexpected quarters. This would be no ordinary western and the opening words of the story are, "This was one of those years in the territory when Apache smoke signals spiraled up from the stony mountain summits..." Geronimo was out to kill.

"Ford had told me about the picture when I'd seen him on the Fox lot. I accepted right away." Ford had bought the rights to the magazine story, 'Stage to Lordsburg', that had impressed him. The producers and financiers had agreed to make the movie but wanted Ford to use big box office names such as Gary Cooper and Marlene Dietrich. Ford held out for his own choices, Claire Trevor and an almost unknown John Wayne. Ford told Wanger "I can get Wayne for peanuts and Trevor is a helluvan actress, and she fits the part." There were to be no outstanding names in the cast line-up. He had asked Trevor if she would make a test with Wayne because he wanted to sell him to Walter Wanger and the studio which was distributing the movie. "I did a test with Duke, who I'd never met before. *He* was testing, not me. Ford had us do the scene after the birth of the baby, about the only real scene we had together. The idea was that he was very respectful of me. He didn't know I was a hooker."

"What a pleasure *Stagecoach* was. Most of the pictures I'd made at Fox were pretty dreary. I went from one to another and we always worked long hours. Then to make a picture with John Ford! Not only did we quit every day at five or six, Ford stopped shooting every afternoon so we could have tea!

"For some reason Ford was interested in me as an actress, I couldn't understand why, because I had nothing at Fox that would have shown any promise.

"You can imagine how thrilled I was when he sent me the *Stagecoach* script. It was a very brief script. Not much dialogue at all. It was terse."

Before the test she had been told Dallas has no first name and no last…Dallas was what they called her when they took the trouble to call her by a name at all. She was a young dance-hall girl who had come from nowhere and was kept moving because she wasn't good enough to associate with respectable women. Dallas is amazed to find herself loved and in love. The important thing about Dallas is her quasi-masculine independence. Nobody owns her, nothing has to be explained to her and she doesn't need protection. Ringo values her toughness and commonsense.

The two female passengers embody the two main film genre types of women; the good girl and the bad girl; the distinction more social than actual since both represented the finest virtues of womanhood. In Ford's westerns women tend to stand for the sacred values of civilization functioning as carriers of culture and fulfilling the essential roles of mother and nurse. Men win this west but women civilize it. Dallas is a bad girl more as a result of bad luck than by choice, orphaned as a child she has been forced to make her living any way she can. Here she accepts her womanly role quite naturally, nursing Mrs Mallory and taking care of the newborn infant.

Trevor is compassionate but her attempts to comfort are initially rebuffed by the gentlewoman. Dallas considers herself to be inferior to the good girl but Ford illustrates that the only difference between them is one of circumstance. Dallas might aspire to some of Lucy's status, but if she is to survive in the West, Lucy needs some of Dallas' strength. Though an outcast in terms of Eastern standards, Dallas and Ringo are the passengers best suited to survival in the West. Products of the frontier, their outcast status results from hardships imposed on them by the uncivilized wilderness. Once Dallas has confessed her sins to Ringo she is cleansed and she can be re-born in a life at his side.

Dallas was explained to Trevor who agreed to do the test with Wayne, "I said 'Sure.' I had never met Wayne or even heard of him. He was a friend of Loretta Young's and his wife was in with all that group. We rehearsed a scene from the picture and shot it, the one where we're standing against the railing outside the inn where the baby was born and we're talking about our history, our past – that tender scene. It was a good test I guess because it sold Wayne to Wanger and the part of Dallas was handed to me."

She had been making pictures for six years and by the time she accepted the role of Dallas, the frontier trollop-with-a-heart-of-gold, she was already considered by many to be over-the-hill and that it took a director of Ford's stature to rediscover her talent. He had seen something special in her that other casting agents seemed to have missed. But the exemplary show piece that was later hailed as his masterpiece provided Trevor with a chance she had long deserved. She grabbed it with both hands and excelled.

It was not her first Western but in this one she shared top-billing alongside John Wayne and earned a salary of $15,000, and Ford, of course, had the happy knack of creating stars. His choices were once again validated in *Stagecoach*, which turned out to be one of the best Westerns ever made and became one of Trevor's own personal favorite and most memorable roles.

"Ford got the most out of us. I was mesmerized by him. He had a kind of radar. He'd say, 'You know, Claire...you can't...that fellow isn't...'" and I'd reply, 'Yeah, I know.' It all became very clear to me."

Later, Ford himself felt her performance in *Stagecoach* went largely unnoticed by the critics because she was so subtle in it. "At the end of the first rough cut, he told me that. He and I were good friends. We had a rapport. He said, 'It's going to be great. And you are so good in it, they're not even going to realize how good you are'. That was a big compliment. And he didn't give them out often.

"He had terrible habits, but a fascinating man! You never knew what was going to be said. But he was so complimentary. Prior to making *Stagecoach* I'd seen him on the Fox lot and he'd say, 'I got a picture for you.' He never told me what or anything, but he did keep me in mind for many years before we got together."

"He was very rough but he and I had a funny kind of relationship, in that he was not very explicit or he could never finish a sentence…unfinished thoughts and I would dig it right away. I found that very exciting. He sort of had a key and opened a door, and that's all he did, and you see it."

"I never thought Dallas was so bad. She was such a good hearted girl. But she had a shady past – the women drove her out of town."

The storyline had brought condemnation from film censor Joseph Breen who reported to Wanger, "The present version seems to be in violation of the Production Code in the following respects: The characterization of your sympathetic feminine lead as a prostitute." Ford agreed to make no specific reference to prostitution and that Trevor would be characterized as an undesirable woman who regenerates. They both agreed that "It pays to be bad when you've got a heart of gold."

Trevor explained, "It's ironic, but audiences seem to like bad girls because they have more character than good girls.

There's always more drama in a woman fighting to right her wrongs than there is in one who finds it easy to be good in the first place."

Trevor unhesitatingly termed director John Ford a genius who knew exactly what he wanted and how to get it. "He could be hard on actors. He was ruthless with Wayne who took a lot of beatings and embarrassment from him. One day he grabbed Duke by the chin and shook it saying, 'You don't act with this, you act with your eyes.' Duke just took it, but in those days he was just getting started. It was embarrassing but boy, it worked. Duke had been making B movies and even Cs. Of course he was very athletic and could easily do the big stunts.

"Ford would get mad. He didn't like any pretense or frills. I remember on *Stagecoach* there was a scene where I'm trying to get Duke out of there, put him on a horse and send him away to escape, and just before he gets on the horse we had a cute little scene, kind of romantic thing. It meant a lot to me and I thought it was going to be great. We get on set and Ford said 'What's this?' He read the scene. He tears it out of the script and says, 'It's too mushy.' He did the scene by just an exchange of looks between us – that's picture making."

Ford had wanted the romance between Ringo and Dallas to be a visual thing, "He set it all up with close-ups. A close-up of me looking at him, then a reverse shot of him looking at me, all done without a line. There was such power in it." Ford had been a believer in only using close-ups two or three times per movie so these really meant something special. Cutting dialogue was Ford's way of getting to the essence of a scene. Trevor said, "He promoted more sex that way and I thought those close-ups were filled with better sex images than they show today when you see two heaving bodies. That's not sexy at all."

Although she was still making the radio show and commuting between the set and CBS and running late all the time, Ford always took precedence, "I'd get hell for being late at CBS and I developed an ulcer from that."

"But the whole thing was a joy to me. It was absolute lush, plush pleasure compared to all the other pictures I'd been making with the eighteen-day schedules.

"We stopped for tea every afternoon. The whole cast was brilliant, the script was so brilliant – not one extra word – and it was just the joy of my life to work on it.

"I wish it had gone on forever. If Ford had said, 'Claire, walk to the edge of the cliff and jump off,' I think I would have done it. I had such confidence in him.

"He was not really verbal in his direction. He would give you the feeling of how he wanted you to play a scene. He would do it with gestures. I got a sort of radio message from him, an electronic exchange between people. So we had a very good relationship. Only one time I remember I came on set and they were shooting somewhere. But the red light wasn't on and I was whistling. Ford yelled out, 'Who's that? Stop it." And I kept on whistling. I thought he was joking and he got furious. That was the only time he screamed at me. He would scream for a lot of things – he was a nervous, high-wire man."

She said that all the crew was friendly and that they came to feel like family, "We were together all the time, because we were in the stagecoach all the time. We were all called at the same time, worked closely together and came to respect each other's talents."

"We had the ordinary amount of rehearsal. I don't think it was overdone but it was well-planned and beautifully directed. I didn't go to the scenes that were filmed in Monument Valley. Only those that were on top who were seen had to be there so I missed the gorgeous country."

"The interiors were shot in Wanger's studio which was also Sam Goldwyn's studio in Santa Monica."

"I think it's the best film I did and the best example of a motion picture. There's no other medium that could capture all that. To me, it's a perfect motion picture."

Although *Stagecoach* is remembered as the movie that made John Wayne a star, it was equally significant in Trevor's own career. In fact in *Stagecoach* and the next two pictures she shot with Wayne, *Allegheny Uprising* (1939) and *Dark Command* (1940), she was billed in the credits above Duke.

She became great friends with Wayne and some of her most memorable performances during this period were opposite him as studio bosses attempted to create a romantic team. In fact both went their own ways after *Dark Command* until over a decade later when she again co-starred with him and gained her final Oscar nomination for *The High and the Mighty.*

She later said of him, "He was a much more complex character than he might have seemed. My God, if you were his bridge partner you had to be on the ball."

She had also enjoyed working alongside Thomas Mitchell as Doc Boone, "Wasn't he brilliant?"

She had been thrilled with *Stagecoach*, "I expected it to be a good picture, but I didn't expect to be swept up and carried along with such joy. I was overwhelmed by this picture. I thought it was the best thing I'd ever seen. I'll never forget the preview of *Stagecoach* because I sat riveted. Usually, I can't look at myself on the screen but this time I forgot I was in the picture. The whole thing was so electric to me – the music and the way it started, the motion of the picture…I was so caught up in the story that I forgot I was in it and I was thrilled to death with the whole thing. When I was leaving the theatre, Jimmy Starr, who was a reporter said, 'That's a damn good Western.' I almost hit him right in the face. To me it was a symphony, a marvelous piece of work that used the motion picture camera in the best way that I'd ever seen it done. It used the medium so perfectly, that it couldn't ever have been that good in any other medium. I wouldn't have called it a western somehow just because it had a western background."

Movie critic Louella Parsons raved, "Yes my friends, theatre owners all over the country have been begging for good old movies and Mr Wanger here gives them all the ingredients for a box office bell-ringer." She added, "Here are three performances that will bring joy to the heart of any audience. First is Claire Trevor, a trouper from her head to her toes…How she plays the girl snubbed by all the women. What a fine job John Wayne does…and then there is Thomas Mitchell."

Variety labeled *Stagecoach* an "exemplary picture."… "All departments work together for distinguished results."… "Claire Trevor handles the frontier trollop with impressive sincerity and dignity."

The Hollywood Reporter of 2nd March 1939, heaps praise on Trevor and Wayne, "They do one grand job of the love interest and make it better than legitimate – they make it something for which an audience can root."

The Hollywood Spectator previewed the film, "Claire Trevor, as the prostitute, earns our instant sympathy and retains it throughout, her performance being the most penetrating she has to her credit."

Nick Clooney wrote in American Movie Classics in September 1995 that he loved "the broken cadence of the brilliant Claire Trevor who set the standard for the western bad girl with a heart of gold."

The movie ultimately rescued John Wayne from making cheaper westerns but it sentenced Trevor to years playing good-hearted-whore roles. "*Stagecoach* made John Wayne a star, but it didn't do much for me. There are certain parts that command attention. I had mine in *Dead End* and *Key Largo*. But not *Stagecoach*. It was too subtle."

Louise Platt, who played Lucy Mallory, said in 1999 that she felt *Stagecoach* was Trevor's picture, "I thought she was wonderful in it. One of my favorite scenes occurs after my character gives birth and Trevor came out holding the baby and says, 'It's a little girl.' That scene was so beautifully lighted with her eyes sparkling and she did it so beautifully. You know she's going to be a warm mother and wife and any man would be lucky to get her – and it's just that one line. To me, that's magic."

Trevor herself laughs at the memory of Wayne walking down the hallway after the birth to rendezvous with Dallas, "Louise Platt said at the time, 'I think he has the most beautiful buttocks I have ever seen'."

For Trevor filming was over all too soon, but she had simultaneously been working on her more unusual and developing Film Noire roles, and in the same year that *Stagecoach* premiered she made *I Stole a Million*; produced by Universal and directed by Frank Tuttle. She co-starred with George Raft in the picture scripted by Nathanael West who had anticipated the whole "noir" genre.

Raft was a gangster attempting to go straight after being forced into a life of crime after losing his life savings. He eventually returns to crime when his wife, played by Trevor, is thrown into jail for shielding him.

She enjoyed working with Raft commenting that he was exactly what she had expected him to be. He always had a bodyguard, Mack Gray with him. She said he was full of fun and very stylish, not a great actor, but a good dancer. "He told me that when he started dancing in New York nightclubs he wore wire shoelaces to keep his shoes on tight. He said he worked so hard his feet would bleed."

This was a big budget picture with many sets and locations. Despite new endings and retakes being shot the movie came in $17,000 under its $349,315 budget. The producers did not expect to pay Trevor any extra salary for her one day extra work, although they did compensate George Raft.

Allegheny Uprising or *The First Rebel* (1939) saw her again teamed with John Wayne for RKO and directed by William A Seiter. This was an ambitious and expensive picture based on the factual story, The First Rebel by Neil H Swanson and it should have been a popular piece of entertainment, starring two of America's newest stars together again after their initial success. There was a determined move to build Claire and Duke as a team to capitalize on the success of *Stagecoach*. Trevor said, "They tried but the pictures that followed were just crumby. *Allegheny Uprising* was a smeared movie. Great cast, good idea, but the production numbers that they shot went on and on forever, and they didn't dare cut one you know, so you have a camera fixed on a bunch of soldiers marching. Who cares? Static.

"It was a child's story of the Revolution. It wasn't very sophisticated or adult." She felt that the film was messed up by not paying enough attention to the personal story, "But I never forgot that RKO built a whole town out in Thousand Oaks for the picture and that we all lived there for six weeks instead of going into the studio."

She said she felt out in the wilderness although they were only about half an hour away from the studio. "It wasn't a hardship living there. We each had our own tent with a bedroom, bathroom and living area. The street was composed of two rows of these tents built along a dirt road.

"While we were there Wayne got news about the birth of his fourth child. How we celebrated. It was the only time I ever saw Duke waver from the straight and narrow as far as his acting was concerned. The next day he had to shoot, but he'd been up all night. He'd been strolling up and down the street carousing."

"I went on a personal appearance tour after that picture. Duke was supposed to be with me. He flaked out and said 'No, I'm not going on that one!' So I ended up alone. My mother came to join me in Pittsburgh and the ladies there were dear to me…It was a thrill. We had a parade down the street with the mayor." She admitted she felt worked like a dog.

"My agent went to South America for six months after *Stagecoach* was finished, and nothing happened." She says she sat around miserably waiting for her next work to come in.

Allegheny Uprising was considered a flop by many reviewers who panned it as "talky" with not enough movement. It was generally considered more of a vehicle for Wayne than for Trevor despite the fact she personally came out of the reviews quite well.

The Hollywood Reporter, 10.21.39 called the movie "A dud" and that "the draggy yarn sinks cast and director." "What might have been stirring film drama of that milestone in American history is just an unimportant incident that will soon be forgotten."

However the article did think that both Wayne and Trevor did their best, making a valiant effort to overcome the handicaps placed on them. "Miss Trevor provides occasional comedy relief."

But the damage was done; she had made one huge step forward with one movie and taken it back again almost instantly. All too soon, she had retreated to playing second fiddle once again to the likes of Lana Turner and Hedy Lamarr and was cast back into the long line of pioneer girls in Westerns.

She hadn't quite finished with adventure although she was now perceived to be taking more center stage roles in her Noire performances. She had been signed by Republic to work with Wayne again on their next big-budget A-movie, *Dark Command* (1940).

She had the talent to handle anything thrown at her effortlessly but producers increasingly considered her to be more at home in the pictures that had a theme of dark fatalistic despair and social criticism. It may well have been that they saw few other actresses who tackled them as well as she did. It may well have been that few other actresses wanted to play depraved or flawed characters. Perhaps they had better agents, more intent on finding them material that they wanted to work on. Whatever the reason, it left the Noire field wide open for Trevor, who found plenty to do as the dark mood reappeared time after time in the pictures of the war and post-war years. She had starred in them from the earliest examples and now became a central figure in the genre.

It would be difficult to suggest that she was typecast in film noire because she seemed to be perfectly able to alternate her style at will to suit the work offered to her. However, retrospectively, it is probably where her talent is best remembered. Even *Stagecoach* itself, had something of the Noire about it; with its dark, brooding atmosphere, the claustrophobia seen on the faces of the inhabitants of the stage, and the lurking dangers of ill lit streets where Ringo faces his own demons and Dallas lives.

Her professional life had become a rollercoaster of wild ups and depressing downs. Her personal life too was beginning to show cracks as Trevor and Andrews began having occasional arguments, "I told him to burn the radio. He kept putting on the war news and it got to me."

At the Top

Trevor was now moving into her most productive and busy period, starting with *Dark Command,* directed by Raoul Walsh. She played Mary McCloud opposite Duke's Bob Seton. Walter Pidgeon starred as Will Cantrell, a character loosely based on the real life Confederate guerrilla leader William Quantrill (spelled Cantrell on the cast list), an educated but bitter man out to take what he could. Wayne was the wandering cowboy attempting to stop Cantrell. Both men love Mary and Roy Rogers starred as Trevor's brother, Fletch.

When Seton arrives in Lawrence, Kansas he quickly falls under the spell of Mary McCloud, daughter of the local banker. Politics is in the air however and in a period just prior to the civil war, there is already a division in the region as to whether it will remain slave-free. When he gets the opportunity to run for marshal, Seton finds himself up against the respected local schoolteacher, William Cantrell. Not is what it seems however. While acting as the upstanding citizen in public, Cantrell is ambitious and prepared to do anything to make his mark and his fortune. After losing the race to become marshal, he forms a group of raiders who run guns into the territory and rob and terrorize settlers, eventually donning Confederate uniforms. It is left to Seton and the good citizens of Lawrence to face Cantrell's raiders in one final clash.

Long before the picture ever went into production Joseph Breen was on the case, warning that the censors would not look kindly on a movie about a 'brutal murderer with not the slightest suggestion of a redeeming quality about him.' Even the State of Kansas House of Representatives was up in arms, commenting, 'Quantrill was an outlaw of the very lowest type and nothing should ever be done to immortalize him.'

Like Cantrell, Quantrill was born in Ohio, taught school in Lawrence, Kansas, became a guerrilla fighter on the Confederate side and burnt Lawrence to the ground. However, the Confederacy eventually disowned him because of his barbarity, executing prisoners, massacring civilians, looting and raping. The real Quantrill was killed in an ambush, beheaded by a Union cavalryman's saber, in Kentucky instead of at the hands of Bob Seton.

Eventually, and with the name spelled differently, the script did pass the National Board of Review, although it was noted by Republic Pictures that whilst some of the incidents in the photoplay were based on real life, all of the events and characters portrayed in the movie were fictitious.

Republic also found itself in trouble for some of the stunts shot for the picture, particularly those involving horses, including the 'seven Running Ws' (a stunt that was later banned), and a water slide that two horses had to descend.

Despite the problems, Trevor was once more in her element, filming on location with friends and a director she clearly respected, "Raoul Walsh was the most casual director I'd ever worked with, he would shoot a scene and turn his back while it was being done.

"Wayne was improving with every picture and he was very sincere. You can't help falling in love with guys like that, but Wayne's fourth child had just been born and I was married so there was no off-screen interest. By falling in love with him, I mean having a crush on him.

"That was a fine history of Quantrill's Raiders. Walsh was very impersonal. Very often he'd say, 'Now we're going to do this scene.' Very cold. He'd sit down, 'You know what to do.' And sometimes when the camera was rolling, he'd turn his back and walk away. But that was his style and he cared, I know. I don't know why he acted like he didn't."

The fact that Mary McCloud had actually lived and loved the two men and changed the pages of post-Civil War history meant she had been considered a "bad" woman, so once again Trevor had to do what she could to convey the complex personality of such a woman who loved so unwisely.

Trevor had been ill over the Christmas period and the picture had closed down to wait for her to return. The delay cost Republic $25,000. Walter Pidgeon had also been ill for several days but Walsh managed to shoot around him.

Reviews of *Dark Command* weren't particularly favorable with some suggesting the picture was pretentious and rather than the acting of its stars winning favor, it was the action and the drama that won the day. "Frankly I thought the excellent cast is lost against the stirring background. Claire Trevor is an excellent actress but the romantic note that she carries seems unimportant in the melee of action." (Plays Film 4.5.40).

Despite the problems the studio faced regarding the stunts, the portrayal of Quantrill himself, along with bouts of sickness, the movie did win some more favorable reviews including one from Film Daily, "Exciting, finely directed historical saga which is sure Box Office in all situations. The action is swift, interesting and of a quality that which urges the onlooker to the edge of the theatre chair."

Before shooting commenced, everyone had been hoping for great things from *Dark Command* and it was Republic's most costly effort to date. Certainly some reviews made it a worthwhile bet with Hollywood Reporter mentioning that "John Wayne more than fulfills all previous promise, while opposite him, Claire Trevor, too, scores with a superlative performance."

Variety was even more gushing, saying that here was a movie that set new standards of excellence. "Claire Trevor delivers a superlative performance as the arrogant maid. Miss Trevor's fine enactment is all the more praiseworthy because of the handicaps of illness she suffered during the filming."

Sick days aside, Trevor was working comfortably through Westerns and Film Noire at the same time; she could just as easily turn an accomplished hand to romance and lighter comedy. The studios however remained unsure how to promote her to the fullest advantage and couldn't make up their minds whether to cast her as good or bad. Producers were possibly less interested in her acting talent than in the promotion of a money-making star. In 1937, in her rebellious period just after she left 20th Century Fox, she had stated publicly, "I want to be bad." Like most film stars of the day, she didn't really have much say in the matter and she was thrown between playing sweet young women to the most depraved drunks.

Whilst studios preferred to have a clear cut delineation that was easy to promote from one picture to the next, building a star image as they went, Trevor herself never felt easy about becoming type-cast. In many ways, because she *could* play any character, she would; employment of any kind paid her bills and to a large extent she was just happy to find work flooding in. But her talent meant that casting directors would seek her out any time they had a potentially difficult role to fill and nobody, least of all herself, concentrated on creating her own celebrity persona.

Trevor herself was one of the most liked people in Hollywood, considered by producers as good-natured and intelligent. She never priced her talent extortionately high and she was readily available. She was however reserved and shunned the social scene preferring to host small dinner parties. Outside her performance, she was less easy to promote.

John Wayne never looked back after *Stagecoach*. John Ford had taken him under his wing and he was happy to build on the image Ford created for him. He fitted the role naturally and gracefully. As this was established over the coming years he rarely ventured far from the isolated individual who put injustice right. That was what his fans wanted to see, what the studios wanted to promote, and maybe even what Wayne was. He developed his own style as a reactor. But Trevor was an actor of the highest order and her path, although it frequently crossed his, was less direct after the breakthrough movie she shared with him and before she had time to glance round, after *Stagecoach,* she was back once again to doing good work in other people's pictures. To begin with producers and casting agents could remember nothing but Dallas and Trevor commented, "Whenever they want a bad girl they call me. In fact, I never thought Dallas was so bad. She was such a good-hearted girl. She just had a shady past." She felt frustrated and said, "I felt like a horrible failure."

After *Dark Command* Trevor decided to take a year out but she remained in high demand and was soon back starring as cute and good in Columbia's *Texas* for Harry Cohn. "I signed a contract with Columbia for two years."

She said Cohn was fine with her even though he had the reputation of being difficult. He wanted her to work on a lot of his upcoming projects but she told him, "I can't, they're so horrible. I've done a lot of bad pictures, but Harry, I can't do this." He tried bribing her with perfume and gifts, "He'd pull out a big bottle of perfume and say, 'Do the picture.' I didn't." But he never docked her pay and she appreciated him despite several run-ins and she usually did whatever was asked of her. "I would have preferred the kind of dramas that Bette Davis had…anything that had real body to it. But while I was at Columbia I got trapped in westerns again. They were inconsequential pictures and they didn't set anyone on fire."

Texas was directed by George Marshall. When two young Virginians, William Holden as Dan Thomas, Glenn Ford as Tod Ramsey are heading for a new life in Texas, they witness a stagecoach being held up. They decide to rob the robbers and make off with the loot. To escape a posse, they split up and don't see each other again for a long time. When they do meet up, they find themselves on different sides of the law. This leads to the increasing estrangement of the two men, who once thought of themselves as brothers. The hostility deepens when thy both fall in love with Trevor.

As was often the case during his career, Holden shaved his chest before appearing, shirtless, in this movie's prizefighting sequence.

From cute and sweet in *Texas* she was immediately back to playing bad and drunk in *Honky Tonk* (1941), an MGM production directed by Jack Conway. She starred as "Gold Dust" Nelson opposite Clark Gable and alongside Lana Turner, as one of the hardest of dames swilling whiskey as Gable's hustler pal.

Like everyone else, she enjoyed working with Clark Gable, "He was like a young boy, cute, unpretentious…I really liked him. As for Lana, she was young and absolutely beautiful. She was easy to work with and she got along with everyone on set."

She was working with the biggest names in Hollywood but she felt this movie was typical of her luck and she later bitterly recalled, "I had some great scenes…at least I thought I had until I went to the press preview of it. My scenes had been scissored out. 'Where am I?' I kept asking myself as I watched it on the screen. 'What happened to me?' I cried all the way home and swore I'd never make another picture. There were a lot of nights I felt like that."

Many things annoyed her about the making of *Honky Tonk*, including the fact that she had to wear brown powder in her hair to distinguish her from the blonde Turner. "I thought it made me look terrible and I felt inferior.

"I was so heart-broken. I thought, I hate this business. I hate it. I'm through. They had cut some of my best scenes out." Trevor believed it was Conway who was partly to blame and she said, "He was sweet. I thought he was a bit lightweight compared to a lot of other directors. I don't think he was a big talent."

At first she was angry, but when she thought her career might be over she admitted, "After that I got frightened."

Needless to say although the reviews of the movie were good, not many even mentioned her. Louella Parsons thought the picture was too long and could easily have been speeded up; little did she know it would have been even longer if Trevor's role had been retained. "There are too many situations that are exaggerated and there is too much repetition...." But sharp eyed Parsons had spotted Trevor and wrote, "One thing you must say for MGM and that is that every character in their movies is always so admirably cast. Claire Trevor is very good as the dance hall girl who has always been in love with Clarke."

Variety's reviewer wrote, "Claire Trevor is in what is now a standard part for her. As a gambling room hustler and dealer she's tops and the inflection she puts into calling her ex-sweetheart Gable, 'Candyman' will get a chuckle."

Her next contract picture for Columbia was *The Adventures of Martin Eden* (1942). Directed by Sidney Salkow, Trevor was again working with Glenn Ford, this time in a sea faring tale.

Columbia loaned her out in 1942 to MGM to make *Crossroads* and later to Paramount to work on *Street of Chance*. Both movies marked her stunning entrance into the dingy sets of Film Noir. Between 1942 and 1950, when she worked on her last, *Borderline,* her work largely lay within the genre and she played every conceivable type of 'bad girl' with conviction. These would be the parts she became renowned for and brought her another taste of real stardom.

The period happened to coincide with worldwide crisis, corruption, atomic bombs, concentration camps, hopelessness and pessimism. Noir movies were a distinct product of those times and represented the surreal view of the world shared by most, where nothing seemed to make much sense. French film critics had been the first to notice the dark mood submerged in much of Hollywood's post-World War Two production. They'd had no access to American films under German occupation but after 1945 came to appreciate them greatly but it wasn't until the 1970s that the term 'Film Noir' began to be heard outside France. Certainly the top American studios of the forties and fifties failed to recognize what they had and Paramount, Fox, MGM and Warner Bros all tended to relegate their crime films to B units and release them on the bottom half of double bills. Other smaller companies released the black and white thrillers relentlessly, although most of these classics were derided by the critics at the time as mere 'guts and gore'.

The roots of Noir were diverse, drawing heavily on detective fiction from Hemingway to Zola and the distorted expressionism of German productions. Each film was full of odd camera angles, a delicate, menacing use of light and symbolic designs and most were directed by European émigrés escaping the horror of war. Despite the critics, they found a massively receptive audience in Depression-hit America.

Crossroads (1942), Trevor's first step into the dark, contained two of the most important noir themes; 'the haunted past' and 'the fatalistic nightmare'. It was a suspense thriller remake of the French film, *Carrefour* (1938), directed by her least favorite, Jack Conway, about an amnesia victim's uncertainty about what had happened to him. Again she was acting opposite William Powell another of Hollywood's fast rising stars. Powell, a diplomat being blackmailed for crimes he wasn't sure he had committed, seeks concealment in dark alleys and dimly lit rooms.

Since John H. Kafka was in Hollywood in the 1940s and even wrote some MGM films, it is not known if his onscreen credit for original story is based on his direct contribution to this film, or was due solely to his work on the original 1938 French version.

Although the story takes place in 1935, all of the women's fashions and hairstyles are strictly in the 1942 mode.

Regardless of the error, the movie earned good reviews and again Trevor was singled out for notice although the LA Examiner only saw her as "Supporting Cast" she was considered, "Grade A" and so good that she lent a great deal of distinction to the story.

Once again she was uncomfortable working under contract and admitted "It's a lot of effort. It seems so natural for me to be bad. It comes easy to me. Everybody raves about my acting. I hadn't even realized I was doing anything unusual. They do me more good than sweet young women. But I don't want to be typed. If the producers had their way I'd soon be the Lucrezia Borga of the West coast. But I don't know why I bother. Believe me it's more fun to be bad. All I have to do is lounge about. Maybe I'm just lazy. I like lounging about."

In March 1942 Trevor admitted her marriage was in trouble and she confirmed she and Andrews were living separately, "He moved out of our home and we are having a trial separation. If, in another month, we feel our parting has been a mistake, we will be reconciled, but if we feel we cannot make a go of it, we'll end the marriage. Neither of us wants to take a definite step until we are sure."

Throughout the three year marriage there had been constant rumors that all was not well, with Andrews often staying out late at parties and frequently seen with his arms round different women. Trevor had always denied the stories until he finally confessed to her that he couldn't be happy with just her and left home.

She told the Press, "There's no use trying to live like that."

In the divorce court she told Judge Archibald, "He earns $250 a week but spends much more. Moreover, although he is the life of the party when he goes out, when he's at home he plays the radio so loudly I couldn't even talk to him."

Although the definite step was taken and the divorce was granted in July 1942, the pace of her work was relentless as she continued filming *Street of Chance* (1942), a Paramount picture directed by Jack Hively. The story was based on the master of paranoia, Cornell Woolrich's, novel The Black Curtain. It was later dramatized several times on the CBS Radio series *Suspense*. The movie saw her enter the Film Noir genre in a big way and in a major project as killer Ruth Dillon, starring opposite Burgess Meredith. She delivered a fine performance as a deadly woman motivated, not by greed, but by love, to murder. "I didn't mean to kill him. I'm not bad. I'm not a killer." In the doom-laden post-war period it was recognized that women could just as easily become murderers as men and for all sorts of reasons.

Once again, the picture concerned the familiar use of amnesia to trigger Meredith's alienation after he is injured by falling construction material. He discovers a year-long lapse in his life and is wanted for murder and has an unrecalled lover.

Whilst Paramount did use its B-picture unit to make the film, it offered a higher degree of professionalism and technical ability than most productions of the time and it was released as an A movie.

Trevor displayed the first hint of the femme fatale, victim of a society that both empowered and enslaved women, that would serve her so well later.

The New York Times rated her appearance as "sufficient."

Columbia and Harry Cohn considered her much more than sufficient and with no time to breathe she found herself swinging back into the saddle and saloon girl attire, from noir to western, starring now in *The Desperadoes*. Directed by Charles Vidtor, Trevor worked alongside old favorites Randolph Scott and Glenn Ford. She went on some dinner dates with Scott and enjoyed his company following her divorce.

Louella Parsons reviewed the movie for The LA Examiner, "You'd have to be pretty blasé and down on the world and yourself not to get a thrill out of *Desperadoes*, the best rootin' tootin' Western we've had this year.

"I don't want to say it is a super western because that wouldn't describe it. It is one of the old kind that made movies popular, but with the benefit of all the modern equipment.

"Technicolor is mighty good to Claire Trevor. She's right in her element as the Countess, who owns a big gambling house and who is secretly in love with Cheyenne. Claire is a trouper and from the feminine point of view she steals the picture."

Her contract was almost up with Columbia but in 1943 she made *Good Luck Mr Yates*, a lightweight movie directed by Ray Enright and co-starring Jess Barker, Edgar Buchanan in a film about an army reject out to prove himself to the whole town in general and Claire Trevor in particular. The picture hardly raised an eyebrow and was so nondescript that even the critics had little to say about it.

Trevor had met fighter pilot, Navy Lt Cyclos William Dunsmore. Though her professional life was confused, her personal one was definitely on the up. She was working on *Woman of the Town* (1943) for United Artists when she announced that she had secretly married Dunsmore in April 1942 in Tijuana after confessing, "It was love at first sight." Her final divorce papers from Clark Andrews were only received in 1943, but Trevor had obtained an interlocutory decree the year before.

Once she completed the movie directed by George Archainbaud and co-starring Albert Dekker and Barry Sullivan in a western about Bat Masterson and his ill-fated love for Dora Hand, she chose to put her career on hold, and on December 1st 1944 their son, Charles Cylos was born. "From childhood on, I wanted children. Even babies in strangers' baby carriages appealed to me. If the maternal part of my nature hadn't been satisfied, I'd have felt like a failure in life. I consider myself lucky."

In 1945 when she bumped into old friend and film critic Louella Parsons of the LA Examiner she was happy discuss what it was like to be married to a naval officer during the war, and a career woman at the same time. She had taken a year out of movies but now said, "Cy and I talked the situation over. He is stationed in the South and has been moving around the country ever since we were married. I asked him if he wanted me to retire. His answer was a big 'NO' he told me that it was important to keep up my morale, my work and to be happy. None of us knew what was going to happen with the war and he told me he couldn't be with me much even if I did move around with him. I did go to Kansas City when he was stationed there. I tried to cook, but I confess I am a total loss in the kitchen. Now I go and visit him between pictures and it's always another honeymoon. He is a fine person and an understanding one as well."

In 1944 she was back at work with RKO shooting their blockbuster, *Murder, My Sweet*, sometimes known as *Farewell, My Lovely*; a movie later remade in 1975. The second adaptation of Raymond Chandler's novel, is much closer to the source text than the original and starred Robert Mitchum and Charlotte Rampling.

Directed by Edward Dymtryk, she was working with Dick Powell in his first tough guy role, playing the hard-boiled detective, in the complex noir mystery, which has often been referred to as one of the most significant films of the decade. Powell's career had been in a slump but *Murder, My Sweet* worked wonders for him. Once more nothing was done to promote Trevor who played one more scheming femme fatal who resorts to murder to maintain her social position.

"*Murder, My Sweet* was very good but I wasn't crazy about working with Edward Dmytryk as a person. I didn't agree with a lot of his theories, and that colored my feelings for him. He was extremely Left and he didn't believe in the father and mother raising a child. He thought the state could do it better. He sent his son away at age two and a half to a boarding school where he thought he'd be raised properly. ... I couldn't stand him. Always talking about the poor and then as soon as he made some money he became a big capitalist."

One critic termed the picture, "pulse quickening entertainment" and the actress also came in for some real acclaim with Dorothy Manners of the Los Angeles Examiner calling her "a knock out in more ways than one as the lady of easy standards. She looks like a million dollars." Trevor received unanimous critical praise with Manners writing, "It's Dick's picture, but this doesn't keep Claire Trevor from shining brightly in the role of a blonde bundle of dynamite out for no good and a personal danger to practically every member of the cast."

Whilst she stood out in the darker movies, Trevor suddenly seemed to become bored with playing the heavy, no matter how fascinating others perceived her roles to be and there was more of the same in her next four pictures; *Johnny Angel, Crack-Up, Born to Kill* and *Raw Deal*, each of lesser importance than the last.

"I'm being typed again," but at least in *Murder, My Sweet* she didn't have to wear a western corset and felt more comfortable.

If the producers couldn't locate her persona on a regular basis or build a consistent image, neither did Trevor bother herself. Co-star Anne Shirley recalled years later, "I was dying to play a heavy. Then Claire told me she was sick of doing heavies and would love to have done the role assigned to me. Claire and I put our heads together and conspired to reverse the female casting, but it did us no good. She went back to being bad and fascinating and I went back to being good and dull."

In 1944, during her hard work at RKO, Trevor bought a house on Bellagio Road in Bel-Air from her agent, "I bought the house for $50,000 fully furnished. A ready-made house. It was during the war and difficult to buy furniture." The studio gave her a loan to buy the property and then made deductions from her salary. "I hired a couple to look after my new house."

Up to that point she had starred in over fifty films, she had rarely had time to worry about furniture. Like most film stars of the day, she had always lived in rented accommodation. "The furniture was modern and not my choice. Everything reflected the Hollywood forties look. The style of the exterior resembled a French country house... a favorite with the residents of Bel-Air.

"If I had the time the house would not remotely resemble what I bought. I would have preferred antiques and chintz. I kept adding things to soften it up."

Trevor's homely happiness did not last however and she admitted in August 1946 that relations between herself and her husband had become strained. Once again, as with her first marriage, she accepted a trial separation, initially stating, "we haven't made any final decisions."

When the war ended Dunsmoor left the Navy and Trevor said he became cruel. The couple divorced in 1947 with Trevor citing her husband's morose sulkiness and failure to look for work after leaving the Navy as the reasons for the split. "When he came out of the navy he made no effort to find employment. Naturally I felt I had to continue with my work, and even though I did, he belittled it, so I felt I was doing the wrong thing all the time." Dunsmoor had told friends he considered people in her business were insincere and didn't trust any of them.

He didn't contest the divorce and the pair settled out of court with Trevor taking custody of their son.

By December 1947 Trevor was noticed around town with Milton Bren.

Bren had previously been married to Marian Newbert. He had been a member of Bren, Weber, Orsatti, Hollywood screen agents but in 1936 had decided the agency business wasn't right for him and signed a five year production contract with Hal Roach. Additionally he became vice president with a percentage of profits. He'd set his mind on making important features with top directors and stars.

He'd also already begun a successful future in real estate.

In 1945 whilst still making movies for RKO she made *Johnny Angel*. Directed by Edwin L Mavin this was another film noir that saw her teamed again with George Raft. Raft starred as a New Orleans ship captain trying to find out details about the death of his father and crew. Trevor was considered to be convincing as the avaricious wife of the head of the shipping line, Gustafson.

Dorothy Manners in LA Examiner wrote, "George Raft, who picks and chooses his roles with the same care a woman takes in selecting a new hat, comes up with his best performance in a long time. When his character attempts to get help from his boss he finds that he is too busy keeping an eye on his chiseling wife (Claire Trevor – and what an attractive chiseller she is) to be much help.

"Trevor gets most of the best lines as the unfaithful wife and her part is similar to several others she has essayed lately."

Crack Up (RKO) 1946 was directed by Irving Reis. Here Trevor played a more sympathetic noire femme opposite Pat O'Brien, who Trevor later recalled as a "dear man, warm and wonderful off screen."

The movie in which she played O'Brien's supportive romantic interest as he attempted to recover from amnesia, was hailed in the New York Times for its competent performances and in Motion Picture Herald as a suspenseful melodrama.

"I played villainesses in many films but it never entered my mind if people thought I was like the characters I played. If they did that was their hard luck. It never bothered me. You had to make those parts believable and some of them were not written in a way that was true to life. They were the concoctions of a dreaming author so that was the difficulty. Nothing is any good unless it's believable."

She certainly had the ability to breathe life into her characters, to make them believable.

She had been working relentlessly, employed on film after film with very few breaks, starring alongside major stars and for any studio that made her an offer. She was rarely outshone.

In 1946 she shot *The Bachelor's Daughters* for United Artists. The movie was scripted and directed by Andrew L Stone. Rosalind Russell had offered her a role in *The Velvet Touch* and she made four more pictures in break-neck succession, first in the lightweight musical romp about four salesgirls who band together in an attempt to attract wealthy suitors. The movie starred Billie Burke, a star of the silent era.

Trevor played the nastiest of the zany fortune hunters, although she later repents.

Critics praised the movie with Don Vance writing, "Girls, you are going to love this one. It is aimed right at the hearts of the poor, poor working gals... Claire Trevor is perfectly at home in her role."

The characters she was playing still failed to excite her and finally, when she felt she could take no more she concluded she would do better returning to the stage where her heart really lay, and in 1946 she worked in *Dark Victory* with Onslow Stevens at the Laguna Beach Playhouse, *Tonight at 8.30* opposite Joan Fontaine and Philip Merivale and then the lead in Noel Coward's *Family Album* at the El Capitan Theatre.

She returned to Broadway and contracted to play in Sam and Bella Spewack's comedy *Out West It's Different*, co-starring

Keenan Wynn. It opened in Princeton but died before it reached New York. However she went on to open in *The Big Two* at the Booth Theatre alongside Philip Dorn and received rave reviews. The show folded after just twenty one performances

"I suppose it was the finest thing that could have happened to me. The Broadway mirage was gone. I had always said I didn't want to be a movie star, and I had meant it. I woke up to the truth and decided to be a Hollywood star. You have such advantages."

So she was available yet again and was immediately picked up for her second contracted RKO picture, *Born to Kill* (1947). The picture was directed by Robert Wise who wasn't known for his work in noire. The picture's original working title of *Deadlier Than the Male* gave a clue about Trevor's role, where she starred opposite Lawrence Tierney as Sam Wild. She had been handed one of her most striking roles as a woman whose desire for material wealth leads her into an unholy alliance with Sam, a cold blooded murderer and she was given free reign as a depraved woman in the suggestive yarn. Trevor played depraved better than any other Hollywood star and here, as Helen Trent, she created her most perverted noir femme to date with her lack of virtue spelled out early after discovering the bodies of Wild's victims but instantly choosing not to notify the police, "It's a lot of bother – coroner's inquests and all that sort of stuff." Whilst she clearly knows about Sam's crimes she is inescapably drawn to him, saying he is, "Strength and excitement and depravity ... a kind of corruptness." Through his corruptness she is led to her own inevitable ruin.

Trevor commented, "I remember it as one of the best. It was one of Robert Wise's first pictures and he was wonderful. I hadn't worked with many top directors but I thought he was tops. He had great taste and inspired confidence."

Equally, Wise enjoyed working with Trevor and praised her performance saying, "She contributed very much to any scene she was in, was very professional, took direction very well. I particularly appreciated her patience and understanding in working with Lawrence Tierney, who tended to be a bit unstable at times. Claire and I always hoped to work together again but the right project never came along."

The movie was critiqued as a "homicidal drama strictly for the adult trade" and a "sexy, suggestive yarn of crime and punishment." A grim business about a killer, his marriage for money and his extra-marital yens and the reviewers also referred to "More Trevor neuroticism."

LA Examiner reviewed the picture with Ruth Waterbury commenting, "*Born to Kill* is definitely exciting, but so too are arson or marijuana or any other taboo things.

"Claire Trevor is an always solid performer. She is so expert in these shady lady roles that it is a shame casting directors won't admit this is acting – and give her a chance at a diversity of roles."

Born to Kill and *The Bachelor's Daughters* were released within months of each other, one presenting a darkly corrupt view of the world and the other a light frothy musical fantasy. Once again there was the clear dichotomy between good and bad and Trevor, according to reviewers and audiences alike, could hit either mark with unfailing accuracy. Torn between a desire to follow her good impulses and to resist the bad, Claire Trevor was still, it seemed, a big name. Her blonde beauty, sometimes sympathetic, sometimes sinister, lit up the darker, moody works which explored a corrupt, violent society, but equally shone as a beacon in the more optimistic and heroic movies produced for a society that saw itself as a strong, powerful world leader.

And 1948 was proving to be a good year for Trevor, for the movie business and for more optimistic Americans too. She was already on to her sixth picture with *Raw Deal*, a fast rolling gangster melodrama. This Edward Small production was distributed through Eagle Lion, directed by Anthony Mann and had an original working title of *Corkscrew Alley*.

The movie co-starred Dennis O'Keefe, Marsha Hunt, John Ireland and Raymond Burr. O'Keefe played Joe Sullivan who breaks out of jail and is helped in his getaway by his sweetheart, Claire Trevor as Pat.

The Board of Censors had seen original scripts for Corkscrew Alley and noted that the basic story was "completely and utterly unacceptable...and a motion picture developed from the screenplay could not be approved.

"The unacceptability of this story stems from its overall low moral tone. It is a sordid story of crime, immorality, illicit sex and sex perversion, without the slightest suggestion of any compensating moral values."

Disregarding the Board, the movie went ahead and Trevor had a major role with good exposure as an acid-tongued, ill-fated actress, continuing her spate of appearances in Films Noir.

O'Keefe had enjoyed working on what he termed a "semi-documentary film", such as *Raw Deal* because it was shot with a news-reel-like feel and directors liked the stars appearing as naturally as possible and they were photographed with minimum make-up. Whilst male actors welcomed this innovation the female stars didn't take too kindly to it, although of course Trevor was well accustomed to being filmed looking as rough and unglamorous as possible.

Somehow, shooting it as a docudrama got the movie passed the tricky Board of Censors. However, despite the film being a major and unusual effort, the producers were unhappy with the distribution and marketing of *Raw Deal* and box office sales fell far short of expectations. Small didn't believe that Eagle fulfilled their contractual obligation and favored other, less important movies and he urged them to fire up their salesmen and bookers, "Let us in short order bring the *Raw Deal* sales up to where they rightfully should be."

Many thought it might have done better if released alongside another medium budgeter but in any case it met with favorable reviews and Trevor was noted in Variety for her "first rate interpretation of a gangster moll, maintaining a steady sense of strain without going to pieces."

Further rave reviews followed the well-performed and exceptionally well photographed rough and tumble. Reviewed by LA Examiner, Shirle Duggan wrote, "All in all, this is an exciting show. The cast go through their paces in an able and entertaining manner." There was no special mention for Trevor.

Film Daily reviewed the picture as "routine." Motion Picture Daily saw it as "formula" and "uninspired." Showman's Trade Review understood right away that it could only do well if "exhibitors get behind it with smart campaigns." Going on, "*Raw Deal* may not send blasé metropolitan newspaper critics rushing to their typewriters, but it certainly will please the majority of moviegoers. Mann has applied just the right touches to lift it from average to a topnotch drama."

On the whole, whilst the picture fell between the critical commentary, Trevor was almost universally considered to be doing what she did best.

Production notes show that Trevor wasn't paid for any retakes or added scenes. She had originally been contracted to earn $5,000 per week for a minimum guarantee of six weeks, (later cut to five weeks).

If *Raw Deal*, thought-provoking and unusual, had largely failed at the box office, Trevor's next picture would prove to be the picture that sprinkled the star dust liberally.

Key Largo (Warner Bros 1948) turned out to be her biggest opportunity since *Stagecoach*, almost ten years earlier. It was directed and co-written by John Huston, produced by Larry Wald who was noted as the busiest producer in town, and starred Humphrey Bogart, Lauren Bacall, Edward G Robinson and Lionel Barrymore.

Most of the players appear in most of the scenes which proved to be a headache for the producer and director who faced many staging problems.

Trevor earned $30,000, Bacall $39,000. The total cost of production was close to $2 million. Trevor was not paid for rehearsal time or additional publicity recordings or the time she gave for shooting promotion stills.

The complex contract provided by the studio was a mysterious mass of double-jointed words that Trevor actually didn't care much about, "I can't even read them." She admitted, "My lawyer – poor dear, explains the contract to me regularly, or when I sign a new one. I always nod and say, 'uh –huh' and shake my head in all the right places. Then I go out and forget the whole thing."

In the case of Warner Bros, she was only concerned with a one picture deal, "It's short and very simple. I haven't however read it."

Huston had arranged that the stars would have a week's rehearsal on set before shooting began – highly unusual. It had been necessary to iron out staging issues and the pre-production rehearsals were popular with Warner directors as a means toward perfecting camera set-ups and a time saver when the cameras actually began rolling. Nevertheless, Trevor donated many unpaid hours to this particular cause.

Huston shot the whole picture with practically no time lapses by arranging the story to take place in the same period of time as it takes to screen, with only one exception near the end of the picture from late night to dawn the next day. It was not surprising there were staging issues.

Sets, confined largely to the Hotel Largo, were designed by Leo Kuter, who brought in 350 different kinds of tropical trees and plants onto Stage 16 to simulate the Largo area.

It was producer Larry Wald himself who suggested Trevor for the part of Gaye when he wired Huston in November 1947. He termed Trevor a stellar performer whilst many still saw her as a supporting actress. In fact Huston also recognized he needed a good actress for the role of Gaye which was not an easy part but whose effectiveness would greatly increase the excellence of the picture. Her assignment in *Key Largo* proved to be one of the most difficult she had ever undertaken.

Again Warners was forced into a corner by the Production Code Administration which continued to take exception to gangsters and their molls, advising Jack Warner, "The very general low flavor of this story, wherein the principals all operate outside the law, militates against acceptance of this story."

Wald considered the censor was attempting to narrow his range of properties "down to where we can either make a musical or a comedy. It is becoming more and more apparent that each story we try to do faces the same problem – we might offend some vocal minority." He was clearly distressed as a producer that he was being limited in the type of material he could buy that would please the censor. "Must we find *Going My Ways*?

"The Breen office today goes by a production code that was written in 1930. Many important events have taken place since the Code was written. Is it possible that the Code is dated?

"The story we are trying to tell in *Key Largo* is a moral one.

"No wonder the industry is continually being ridiculed.

"This piling up of continuous censorship is what is making all our pictures empty."

One of the issues raised by the censor was the obvious drinking by Trevor's character, but in a later note to Warner, Breen noted, "Character of Hazel must not be kept woman of Muriello...OK to leave her dipso, but reduce to minimum drinking." (Names of characters were later altered.).

By now Trevor had done plenty of good work in bad pictures but in 1948 she stormed into what was to be her last film noire, recapturing lost ground in *Key Largo*. A star of lesser caliber might not have wanted to take the risk that Trevor grabbed with this movie. Her principal female opposition in the film was Lauren Bacall. There was an ever present danger that in such a situation Bacall would get all the best opportunities and she would have to take the best of what was left. The script had also been written by Maxwell Anderson as a tough man's story. The female parts were less than robust.

But Trevor turned in an extraordinary performance as washed-up, boozy nightclub singer Gaye Dawn opposite Edward G Robinson's big time gangster. She stole the show as his long suffering moll who is now a fallen favorite with fading looks and who drinks to forget. Clearly whiskey is now her only solace. Humphrey Bogart is an ex-army officer who thinks he is tough enough to resist Robinson's whole gang.

Each character comes together in Lionel Barrymore's waterside hotel on the Florida Keys. Each cast member jealously guarded their own screen time. But whilst Trevor didn't get too many scenes herself, she dominated every one of them lending her character a tough veneer on the outside whilst hinting at tender vulnerability underneath. Trevor reflected her hatred for the way her lover made his living and Gaye is full of heart-rending emotional conflict.

It was a tribute to her style and magnetism that she held the attention in scenes playing opposite Robinson, Barrymore and Bogart and she deservedly won an Academy Award for her electric performance.

"It was a great part."

From the first moment when, seated at the bar, more than half drunk, she was superb as was her rendition of Libby Holman's Moanin'Low, sung in tuneless desperation for the price of a drink.

Trevor made her motion picture song debut under handicaps that might have discouraged a less courageous actress. In the first place she was suffering from a cold when it was shot and secondly she did it without accompaniment and not in the recording studio, but right on set.

"It's supposed to be bad singing, so I can't lose."

"This was Huston's brilliance. First of all, I had no idea I was going to sing. I thought they were going to have a recording and I was going to mouth the words. I wanted the music department to rehearse me and train me in the gestures of a nightclub singer. I wanted to get that look. Each day I'd say to John, 'When can I go and rehearse, when are you going to shoot the song?' 'Oh we've got lots of time'. This went on and on. We did take time on the picture but it was fun. We'd take an hour and a half for lunch. Bogart and Huston were fun. Electric. I began to really pester John. So we came back from lunch one day he said, 'I think I'll shoot the song this afternoon.' What? Where's the recording? I haven't heard it? He said, 'You're going to sing it.' I can't. Huston and Barrymore both said I'd be fine. And that's what he did to me. He stood me up there with the whole cast and crew looking. You think that's not embarrassing? And off stage is a piano, and they hit one note. Start. No time for anything except pure embarrassment and torture, and that's what came through. I tried to do it as well as I could. And when we'd done the long shot all the way through, I thought I was finished. It was off key I don't know how many times. He said, 'All right, now we'll do the two shot and the close-up,' and the piano would go 'Bong' off-stage and that was it. So each time I did a different set-up and then they had to be blended together, you can imagine how many keys I was in."

But it worked, and she came across like the terrified embarrassed woman she was meant to be, and Huston of course had handled her just right by not rehearsing it.

Trevor was enthusiastic about her role, if not the property itself, "I thought the play was static and the film rather static too." However she agreed she enjoyed the experience of making it, "We all had such a good time; John Huston could tell a story better than anyone you've ever heard. It's odd though, he was highly articulate, yet when he was directing actors he became very unarticulated – never finished a sentence. He'd say, 'You know it's, er, like this' … but the thing was you always ended up knowing exactly what he wanted."

She regarded Huston as a dream to work with, along the same lines as Ford and she said, "There was something intuitive about his direction."

Bogart named the boat that appears in the film the Santana after his own boat.

"There was only one shot taken in Florida with Bogart getting off a bus at the beginning of the picture, but the rest of us never got to Florida. Most of it was filmed at the Warner Brothers studio. We all had two rows of dressing rooms on the stage. We had one whole stage just for the dressing room, we shot on another stage and Huston had a third stage to himself where he had his office and he was reading new scripts. Every day we'd all have lunch at the country club out there. It was a party – it was wonderful."

She'd worked on several projects with Robinson by this time but she said that on this occasion he presented several minor disturbances such as walking into Warner's Research Department to demand a copy of Dickens' Christmas Carol. He walked out reading it and making gestures to himself. When he returned to set, with the book, he forced Lionel Barrymore, famous for his radio Scrooge characterization, to listen to the whole story as read by Robinson.

Critics thought it was strange how she managed to do so well in so many parts that were not the pick. WH Mooring commented in Picturegoer in July 1948, "In fact she can do more on less than any actress I know." He said Lauren Bacall might have got all the best opportunities in the film and with an all-star cast, it was hardly likely that that Trevor would get too much screen time. However she dominated every scene she was in, including the ones where Bogart, Robinson and Barrymore fought against each other. It was a tribute to her style and power that she could hold her own and capture the attention of the audience.

She herself could often be dismissive of her career and of Hollywood, saying that she felt films were not an art but a business and that anyone, given a chance, could do what she did. Of course this took no account of the fact that acting came easy to her. It was instinctive and she never really valued her own talent. She could never see why being an actress should cause so much fuss. To her, it was a job that she did to the best of her ability.

She had never needed particularly well drawn scripts in order to give top performances although in *Key Largo* she had been given a rare part that didn't often arrive in the business.

LA Examiner, Ruth Waterbury wrote *Key Largo* is ambitious and intellectual. Its highly literate script has things to say. You can take it, if you want to, as a fast paced, action melodrama…or you can listen to what its characters say…and get the film's distinctive values. Bogart turns his character into a distinctive human being, but excellent as he is here, he is not in the final analysis the star of this picture. Claire Trevor is…let's face it, the husky-throated Claire has the best part. Her role is as clear in its purpose as a bullet hole, and Claire blazes forth with a performance at once heartbreaking and unforgettable."

Variety: Claire Trevor is standout, giving one of the best performances of her career.

Hollywood Reporter: Trevor's performance is one of those superlative jobs of acting that comes from this performer whenever she is given the opportunity. It is played thoughtfully and intelligently and reaches heights of pathos in the sequence wherein she tries to recapture the days of her singing career.

She won the Oscar for best supporting actress. Trevor said, "Bogie was over for dinner a couple of nights before the Awards and he told me that if I won I should get up and say that I wasn't going to thank anyone, that I did it all by myself. Well when I won it was hard to say anything, it was hard not to cry. Walter Huston had just said in his acceptance speech, 'I hope when I get to be an old man, my son will take care of me', so when I got up there I said, 'Well, I have three boys and I hope they take care of *me* in my old age.'

Trevor and Bogart were already close friends, "I always felt like he was my buddy and I appreciated his humor. I called him 'Bogart' not 'Bogie' and no one called him Humphrey except as a joke.

Trevor was now a 'real' Hollywood star. She had her Academy Award and nothing could ever take that recognition away. She was herself, still skeptical about the industry, "My heart was seldom in my work. I was bewitched by the legitimate stage and regarded Hollywood as a bad joke. But perhaps my indifference to Hollywood wasn't all my fault. More than thirty low-budget B pictures in five years!"

She also believed that her lack of ambition seriously afflicted the early days of her career. She had never ruthlessly gone after parts, "I didn't know that to make a real career in Hollywood you have to become a personality, have to cultivate publicity departments and become known as 'The Ear' or 'The Toe'."

Bing Crosby once confessed to Barbara Walters that he preferred second or third billing in a movie saying, "Stars are gone in a flash, but co-stars just keep working at it." It was a sentiment shared by Trevor, but she was so much more than that.

Mooring had commented in Picturegoer that Trevor never put in a bad performance despite being cast in many a bad film, "too many of them for her own good."

No matter how high she reached, no matter the critical acclaim she achieved, she now took nothing for granted. She had learned the hard lessons of her early career.

Trevor and her second husband had divorced in 1947 and on November 14th 1948 she married producer Milton H Bren who had been her agent when she first left New York. They married at the home of Judge Thurmond Clarke, an old school friend of Trevor's, in Pasadena. Both had been determined to keep the marriage free of fanfare and only a few close friends were present. They honeymooned in California, stopping off anywhere the mood took them.

Although she had known him since her career first started, she hadn't had much to do with him as he handled mostly writers and directors and she was with a different part of the agency.

Eventually, after they had both divorced they met up at a tennis tournament, "We went to Ed Lasker's house after the tournament for dinner and dancing. I danced with him and he was a wonderful dancer."

"I didn't begin my life till I married Milton Bren."

She had been married and divorced twice and had no intention of marrying again, "But we started going out. We had a wonderful time. We went together for two years before we were married because we wanted his children to get used to us being together."

Bren had moved into movies and established his own production company alongside director William Seiter and playwright Norman Krasna.

In 1992 a neighbor of the couple said "It was one of Hollywood's truly good marriages. They shared the sea, the kids, parties, travel. On their last boat they must have travelled 50,000 miles."

Bren had two teenage sons from a previous marriage but they accepted Trevor and they both moved in with the newlyweds, "We were an immediate family, my son and his two boys."

The family settled down before a new baby son, Peter, came along. She and Milton enjoyed a charmed marriage and he referred to her as "the most intellectual person he ever met."

Trevor had never allowed acting to dominate her life and she settled down with Bren, making her family her life.

Bren was a yachtsman so the family suddenly became even closer to the Bogart household. "Bogart loved his boat…I think any man with a yacht loves it more than he loves his wife. We'd spend every weekend in Catalina and we had adjacent moorings in Moonstone Beach."

The families used to race the boats and Bren would always tease Bogart that his boat was so slow he'd give him a head start.

By then Bogart had married Lauren Bacall, "We were with Bogart and Betty all the time. We went to New York together, he'd call my husband 'Miltie'. The whole last year of his life I'd see him almost every weekend. He was in terrible pain in the last year. It got worse and worse. It was a very hard time.

"I started a painting of Betty and wanted to finish it so he'd be able to see it. I'd be over at their house all the time and he was skin and bones. I brought the painting over one day while it was still wet and he looked at it and his whole face lit up. So that was terrific, he loved it."

After she married, Warner Bros producers took it for granted that she was no longer interested in a film career. They were not prepared to bother acquiring anything new especially for her.

She had planned to spend the summer on vacation in New England after completing *Key Largo*, but other studios were eagerly offering new parts. She cancelled and remained in Hollywood to do more film work although for the most part, she considered she was again hired for films that were only passable. "I never got to work again with Wyler, Ford or Huston. But that's life isn't it?"

Now she found herself working on pictures such as *The Velvet Touch* (1948) and *The Babe Ruth Story* (1948). *The Velvet Touch,* an RKO production, was directed by John Gage and starred Rosalind Russell, Leo Glenn, Sydney Greenstreet and Leon Ames.

When renowned Broadway actress Valerie Stanton (Rosalind Russell) decides to leave her ex-lover producer Gordon Dunning (Leon Ames) to do serious drama with a new producer, Dunning threatens her with slanderous actions. Dunning has been the producer of all the big plays Valerie has appeared in for the past 10 years and threatens to poison her relationship with her current beau, successful architect Michael Morrell (Leo Genn). In a fit of rage Valerie fatally strikes Dunning with a bronze statuette, and just by chance fellow actress and competitor Marian Webster (Claire Trevor) is discovered with the body and is held for the murder. Valerie is in shock over her own actions, and when police Capt. Danbury (Sydney Greenstreet) investigates, the tension mounts as the actress' conscience begins to erode her nerves and a game of cat and mouse with the police ensues.

Lux Radio Theater later broadcast a sixty minute radio adaptation of the movie on January 10, 1949 with Rosalind Russell and Sydney Greenstreet reprising their film roles. Again, on August 23, 195, Screen Director's Playhouse broadcast another radio adaptation of the movie with Rosalind Russell reprising her film role.

The black coat Valerie wears to visit Marian, with its hood trimmed in white, was later copied for Kim Basinger in *L.A. Confidential*.

Dialogue in *The Velvet Touch* is some of the first to draw attention on celluloid to Dior's New Look which had become fashionable on the cat walks the year before. As Valerie leaves the theater, an extra is heard to say, "She's got the New Look, it sure suits her."

The title song, with music by Leigh Harline and romantic lyrics by Mort Greene, was sung during the opening and closing credits by an unidentified male chorus. It was an atypical choice for a film of this genre.

The film was produced by Russell's husband Frederick Brisson. It was director Gage's only theatrical venture, the rest of his credits being for television.

Sydney Greenstreet was one great presence in film – literally. In *The Maltese Falcon* he filled every inch of the screen. John Huston shot "The Fat Man" from such a low angle that he actually looked even larger than he was – which was pretty big. At sixty two, this was the first film the proud stage actor had agreed to be in. His film career would only last eight years but he worked with some of the greats in movies. Greenstreet doesn't appear in the film until after the 45 minute mark. Getting to that point in this routine drama is a chore for any movie fan.

The melodrama is considered 'film noir' probably due to the crime, the lengthy flashback at the beginning of the film, and the shadowy shots at Russell's apartment after the killing. Cinematographer Joseph Walker worked on other noir-like films including *The Dark Past, The Lady from Shanghai, Harriet Craig, The Mob* and *Affair in Trinidad*. Unfortunately this is not as dank as most others of the noire genre.

All the Broadway sophisticates talk and behave like they were in a stage play and the two standout performances are from noir regulars Claire Trevor and comical Esther Howard. It's not surprising that they're the only actors in the film to play anyone even close to down-to-earth. Trevor is refreshing as a love-sick but hard-boiled actress who's accused of the crime and Howard is funny as an obsessed Broadway fan. All the men, unfortunately, are lanky, mustached fifty-somethings that every young woman in these types of film seem to find dreamy.

In her next movie, *The Babe Ruth Story* (1948), Trevor starred in a fictionalized biopic about the famous baseball star. Trevor said, "I played opposite William Bendix in *The Babe Ruth Story*. I met Babe and his wife who I portrayed in the movie. Babe wasn't well by then and had lost his voice. He died not long after of cancer."

The plodding production was released by Allied Artists and directed by Roy Del Ruth. As Mrs Ruth, Claire Trevor does standard stuff, but in the pre-marriage scenes she is seen dancing in beaded tights. This was her first non-neurotic role in years.

The film was rushed for release while Babe Ruth himself was still alive. George Herman Ruth lived just 21 days after seeing the premiere that he attended on Monday, July 26th, 1948.

The scenes at Yankee Stadium were shot and filmed, just hours before a real baseball game was scheduled to take place. William Bendix actually hit a ball over the right field fence, (he was the first actor to do so).

Reviews were, for the most part, negative, citing the film's moments of heavy handedness including a contrived re-enactment of Babe Ruth's famous World Series home run against the Chicago Cubs, some critics referred to it as one of the worst sports biopics of all time.

Ruth Waterbury writing in The LA Examiner review however called it a "Fine, touching, entertaining movie." She considered that recent films had lacked heart, were more often than not thrillers and chillers, but that here was real sentiment and warmth, "Sweet as chocolate icing spread on the cake straight from the oven!

"Claire Trevor's portrait of a decent and aspiring chorus girl is most persuasive. There's a wonderful, forthright touch about all Claire's work but it's nice to see her given such a sound person as Mrs Ruth to portray after all the neurotic drunks and slum dames she's had wished on her by stupid casting."

Variety commented on 19th February, 1948, "Claire Trevor, the girl whom Babe pursues, after she puts him straight about himself in his early days of baseball, and who later becomes his wife, once again proves she is a top flight actress when the material is available."

John McCarten wrote more succinctly in New Yorker, "Claire Trevor is equal to the material."

Others commented that Trevor shone as a fine actress who was rarely given opportunity commensurate with her ability but who unfailingly met the highest expectations.

In 1949 she had another chance to shine for United Artists in *The Lucky Stiff*, written and directed by Lewis R Foster and produced by Jack Benny. The movie starred Brian Donlevy, Irene Hervey and Dorothy Lamour.

Semi-successful lawyer John Malone (Donlevy) is intrigued by local night club singer Anna Marie St. Clair. After meeting her at the club, he is present when her boss is killed, and she is arrested for the crime. Sentenced to death, Malone and his faithful secretary set out to find the real murderer, who is probably also responsible for a protection racket Malone is investigating.

Trevor had good exposure as Malone's breezy secretary and the picture received some good reviews, particularly from March 16th 1949 LA Examiner: "Jack Benny let me tell you, you've got a hit.

"Of course Jack, when you signed Claire Trevor you proved you ain't never been no accident in show business. That was real smart signing boy, for here's a gal who never gives a bad performance. Or let's put it this way, she unfailingly gives a good one. As Donlevy's smitten secretary she even gives a fine one."

In fact just as the picture was due to roll Trevor was injured in a car crash on Sunset Boulevard. Although her car was a right-off she refused to go to hospital and instead, carried on to the studio. She was so stiff with bruises she could hardly walk and was eventually sent for X-rays. Doctors said she could continue to work but her lacerated knees were bandaged up and she had to film certain scenes sitting down.

In 1949 critic Len Wallace summarized Trevor's career to date in an article in Picturegoer, commenting that he felt she hadn't reached the top of her profession because she was too good, "I consider that she is one of the most capable actresses on the screen, established stars not excluded. No one in Hollywood has had a career more chequered than hers. She is so good that she will probably never become a top-ranking star." Needless to say Trevor had heard all this before.

In considering her work in *Key Largo*, Wallace had written, "Such brilliant work might well elevate any other girl to stardom, but with Trevor you never can tell." She had been in movies over fifteen years by then and critics and reviewers had consistently been effusive and enthusiastic about her "crackerjack" performances, but despite everything, nothing much had happened in the way of reaching the stars. Wallace despaired of her ever being offered starring roles; everyone it seemed respected her talents in Hollywood but continued to scandalously ignore them. By now, through more than a decade she had been cast in too many bad pictures for her own good; no matter that she shone in them all.

She had steadfastly refused to knuckle down to standard Hollywood convention and didn't seem to accept or respect the mythology surrounding the biggest stars of her era. Her acting talent allowed her to create screen characters with a rare ease and a well-hone technique that seemed like second nature.

She was a laid back personality and made no secret that she believed there was no mystery about good screen acting. Her often quoted opinion was designed to bite the hand that fed her. The whole Hollywood system depended on the mystique of stardom and her philosophy was one that male stars might get away with at that time, but certainly not a female. Hollywood women were supposed to achieve their best results through an inner, unseen inspiration that raised them above the more common place performers. Trevor was too down to earth for any nonsense.

She refused to accept that she was anything special and she often stated that her best work resulted from an intelligent reading of character coupled with her acquired skill. All her work bore out that position. She put together full, rounded characters with dramatic emotional impact. Wallace said, "You feel exactly what she wants you to feel; even the worst drab she has portrayed somewhere pleads with, for and obviously obtains your sympathy – but never cheaply."

She never used the cheap sentimental tricks of her trade. Instead she cleverly created true character, uniquely concentrating her gestures to a minimum for most impactful effect. Everything she did was directed toward a prejudged result. She was not concerned with projecting her own personality into any performance. Trevor had no inner, hidden agenda and she was hugely generous toward other actors.

Her artistic honesty might have been too much for the Hollywood star system. As a supporting actress she could add distinction to ordinary pictures, whilst as a star she would have commanded the very best scripts and production standards since her own talent would illuminate anything shoddy. In fact, just as Ford and critic Wallace said, she was simply too good to be the perfect Hollywood fit.

By the late 1940s Trevor herself may not have cared much either way. She seemed to have her heart and eyes turned back once again toward the New York stage and away from the screens of Hollywood. She longed to return there to a big theatrical success. First and foremost she had always considered herself to be a stage actress. Films gave her easy access to money, but they never stirred her ambition. Occasionally a really good vehicle would come her way and she would have a brief change of heart and ultimately she came to accept that an actress of integrity might find some artistic fulfillment in movies, and maybe had even hoped to reach some level of stardom herself. But she didn't go out of her way to attain it. She stuck to her guns and in consequence was respected and admired rather than adored or deified.

She was rarely introspective however, and tended not to bemoan her situation, instead Trevor maintained her athletic diversions and continued playing tennis, golf and ocean swimming. She considered herself sporty and preferred wearing plain sports clothes to more formal attire.

Throughout her life she was an avid reader and conveyed her enthusiasm through a collection of rare Dickens' figurines. She also maintained her love of art and on set could often be seen sketching fellow workers on set.

As her career developed she also found a liking for the finer things in life and quoted that her favorite dishes were "Lobster a la Newburg" and the hot hors d'ouevres served at the Hotel Marguery in New York.

Her world had changed. She was in love and settled happily into her new marriage. Bren, having shares in a production company, was able to offer her choices seldom previously open to her and he happily widened her horizons.

New Directions

With the advent of the 1950s the actress had continued to perform stellar portrayals in a wide variety of pictures, albeit mostly movies of less than excellent quality. She had just won her Academy Award but many observers still had no idea that a major part of her talent had been smothered under repetitious typecasting.

Now, finally, with Bren in her corner, Trevor was out to prove she could be witty and funny in *Borderline*; the opportunity arising because this picture was partly financed by herself and new husband.

"This was a cute picture and my husband Milton Bren produced it. *Borderline* is very close to my heart because of his involvement in it." She said she worked twice as hard as she would have for another producer, "Work didn't cease with the end of a day's activities at the studio. Driving home we'd be discussing some little item or other which might improve the picture."

The melodramatic thriller *Borderline* (1950) was released by Universal International and directed by William A Seiter. It was independently produced by Milton H Bren through Borderline Pictures which was owned by Bren, director Seiter and star Fred MacMurray. They personally financed what became a family affair. Trevor had some reservations about working on her husband's film, modestly explaining that she thought he should have got someone better.

Bren dealt directly with Nate Blumberg, president of UI, who agreed to take over distribution of the picture. Under the agreement UI handled *Borderline* as one of its own releases worldwide. Bren and Seiter were also consultants along with UI sales executives on the selling campaign for the movie.

The screenplay by Devery Freeman was based on an original story by Norman Krasna and brought together Trevor and Fred MacMurray as two undercover agents who infiltrate a drug-smuggling ring operating between California and Mexico. Neither is aware of the other's identity.

Alfred Ybarra had dressed Santa Susanna airport in the San Fernando Valley to look like a small Mexican airport.

Customs agents search for information about Pete Ritchie (Raymond Burr), who is involved in smuggling drugs into the US. Police officer Madeleine Haley (Trevor) acting undercover in order to gain Ritchie's confidence, soon meets him through one of his associates. As she is talking with Ritchie, Johnny Macklin (Fred MacMurray) and one of his men burst in, and they provoke a violent confrontation. From then on, Haley is in constant danger as she attempts to figure out everything that is happening in the smuggling operation. She becomes the victim of Macklin's ruthlessness and all-round un-gentlemanly behavior. She thinks he is the gangster, he thinks she is a moll.

Trevor fully intended winning another Oscar in this lighter comedy role, giving Madeleine Haley a highly emotional characterization. "Having won an Oscar, I wouldn't mind winning another."

Discussing the difficulty of playing comedy, Trevor said, "Such a simple thing as an onion can make people cry but there's no machine as yet invented to make people laugh. Emotional drama is a pushover in comparison to comedy.

"I'd rather face the most taxing emotional scenes ever written than the tiniest bit of comedy. I work twice as hard to be funny. How I admire comedians like Fred MacMurray. Believe me comedy is a serious business.

"Whenever I'm asked my opinion of what is most difficult about the job of acting I'm usually tempted to reply 'Every and all there is about acting.' It's true that the more experienced the performer becomes, the more they realize that one never stops learning. To my mind there is no complete master or mistress of the acting profession.

"With every role come interesting new technical problems to face or solve. I firmly believe that every artist remains, at heart, a student, constantly inquiring, testing, curious and hopeful that she has done the right thing.

"To me the most difficult phase of acting is listening, whether before the camera or footlights. It sounds simple – to listen and react to what your co-player is saying, but you'd be surprised what a technical feat this is. It's a quicksilver accomplishment that can desert the finest star at any moment."

Trevor was always modest about her ability; she was also constantly questioning her own efforts. She was justifiably proud of her Academy Award achievement, but apparently five-year-old son, Charles, was less so and he referred to it to all his young friends as "Mamma's Monument."

"The Brens are a happy family and we're together constantly. Milton and I believe in old-fashioned home life, breakfast and dinner with the children, a show with the children, good books, friends, lively conversation."

As a good luck token Trevor took to wearing a miniature gold "Oscar" necklace and she had it with her every moment on the set of *Borderline*, "Just to keep the right vibrations."

Trevor had to speak Spanish and had a consistent work out as much of the action took place on the California-Mexico border.

Raymond Burr was one of Hollywood's leading bad men. He had deliberately gained weight to become one of the busiest actors in the business.

When they first started work on *Borderline*, the husband and wife team made a vow not to talk about it when they got home from the studio. The promise was obviously not kept, but they penalized themselves a dollar whenever the film was mentioned outside work hours; the kitty quickly reached $50. An undisclosed final sum was donated to charity.

Trevor had to sing and now also dance to Carlotta, a new melody from Sammy Cahn. At the time of filming Trevor had a sprained ankle following a fall during a scene, but she carried on through eight hours with no delays to filming. Between scenes an attendant massaged her foot and ankle and kept ice packs ready, "I've danced eight hours with only occasional rests. That's equal to the average worker's office day, only they get to sit while I had to stay on my feet. And sore they are!"

Trevor shopped and selected her personal wardrobe, one of the few times a star had been able to do this. She had to choose clothing far from her own taste and during shooting she looked anything but the blonde beauty she was. She had been handed a sum of money by Bren and told to go shopping. She spent a happy week covering the shops, "I remembered to watch the budget carefully. After all, it's my husband's picture so I spent his money wisely."

Trevor spent much of her free time on set sketching portraits and she also illustrated her practical mind during filming a sequence with a parrot (the heroin had been hidden in its cage to be transferred into Los Angeles). She sat laughing as she watched the crew attempting to film the bird which was central to the plot, but which kept turning its back on them. To no avail the crew did everything possible to make the bird turn. Finally she suggested they turned the cage round.

Sadly, Trevor didn't think the picture came out as well as it should, "I don't think Bill Seiter was a strong director and the script didn't click. Seiter wasn't very deep and he had done comedy earlier, but time had passed him by a bit by the time we did the picture. In later years I would often get directors who had passed their peak and were starving for work."

Borderline had its world premiere at the Aldine Theatre in Philadelphia on Saturday January 28th as part of a series of key city openings. Trevor, still hard at work, made personal appearances at each performance.

Following the premiere performances she returned to New York to make several radio appearances to support the picture.

There had been plenty of wrangling about the premiere and other promotional dates and executives at UI were loath to spend too much distribution money, arguing that Trevor, Bren and Mr and Mrs Seiter were all travelling by train for the one public appearance of Trevor, and they argued that whilst the publicity trip would be supported, the amount of radio and television space would be limited and the head of UI considered that *Borderline* was the wrong kind of picture for saturation handling. He felt that Trevor and MacMurray were big enough stars to carry the success of the picture without having a lot of money spent on promotion. He also felt the promotion was taking too much of Trevor's time which he felt could be better utilized.

Trevor wanted to spend two weeks in New York, but UI wanted her to visit other key cities such as Boston, Washington and Chicago. By the end she was exhausted.

A series of minor, comic approach, advertising campaigns were created but the film still did not open well, to the concern of all involved, especially the Brens.

Through January the movie finally did receive nation-wide saturation promotion paid for by UI, and Trevor was handed another hectic schedule of interviews, photo opportunities and public appearances. Bren was told by UI executives to be discreet about expenses and no special entertainment was provided for the party.

She worked flat out on promotion and even found herself doing monologues before live audiences, "When you make public appearances you can do one of three things, you can say how many pretty girls there are in Boston and how glad you are to be here with all these nice people. You can sing songs. I didn't think anyone would want me to do that, so I do a seven and a half minute monologue.

"It's a tragic little thing about a girl who is trying to make a phone call. While she is waiting for the operator to get her the number she thinks out loud. There are no props, not even the telephone. I'm just a little nervous."

She was tiring and said, "Hollywood people are always 'on'. They're as much a part of the average household as was washing powder or salad dressing. The public, which put a celebrity where he or she is, has a perfect right to indulge its curiosity. That doesn't mean a star must live for her following.

"But it does mean that those in our business must consider the fans are responsible for their very existence and make room for them in their thoughts and actions."

Trevor and Bren chose to remain close to the fireside and didn't often go out to night clubs and this meant that, outside the promotional tours, she had fewer brushes with her fans than most, "In Hollywood I can go anywhere I want and meet the most orderly, friendly sort of people who take me for granted because of being used to seeing picture people in person.

"It's in New York I have my skirmishes with crowds and I must admit they are rugged. I'm so afraid people will get hurt in the crush. When it's over and I'm satisfied all is well, I breathe a sigh of relief."

She went on "I'd be an unhappy girl without this attention. It's a barometer of how I'm doing as an actress. Motion picture people stand as symbols to a great many people."

She did say however that many of her fans made the assumption, based on many of her movies, that she was unlucky in love, "If anyone could develop a neurosis on the subject, I could from receiving so much sympathy on my failures in love. I never before realized how seriously the public takes its make-believe. It's all too fantastic. I must do something about the letters. After all, a girl's got her pride and I must convince these well-meaning people that I'm merely the victim of the script writer."

In *Bordeline* she finally got to keep the man and she laughed, "Just to prove I can. It isn't as much fun portraying the marrying kind. Street girls seem to be more colorfully written."

In a five minute interview pre-prepared by Borderline Pictures for the Press Agency she added that she didn't mind what she'd been doing in pictures but went on, "I'd better start getting my man."

On October 8, 1951 Lux Radio Theater broadcast an adaptation of the movie with Trevor and MacMurray reprising their film roles.

After the original 1950 copyright lapsed in the 1970's, the film was considered to be in the public domain, and so found its way into the inventory of countless independent videotape and DVD distributors.

Early reviews of the picture were not good including one from Film Daily on January 12th which read, "Serious plot misfires into silly spectacle. Should have been played for laughs. Tries hard. End result is just fair. Direction – Awkward. Photography – Good." It went on, "Two good players seem to have approached the script as a job that must be done."

Motion Picture Daily; "A distinctly routine adventure film. Nothing appears to have been contributed to entertainment values by focusing attention on dope in this picture. Performances are adequate."

Variety; "Spotty entertainment values in this pic stem from its indecisive treatment as either a straight comedy or a serious meller...customers won't know whether to laugh or bite their nails. Likelihood is that they'll do neither since the total impact is mild."

LA Examiner 13th Feb 1950; "*Borderline* can't quite make up its mind whether it's a slapstick comedy or a chase thriller but it offers some excitement and some laughs. Miss Trevor plays up to her embarrassing situation with pep and plenty of personality." Earl H Donovan continued that Trevor's personal performance was delightful.

Louella O. Parsons wrote in Cosmopolitan in March 1950 that *Borderline* was done with "Spritely showmanship and kept sparkling with such lively suspense that it is completely ingratiating.

"Welcome to the very small ranks of our important comediennes, Claire…we need more like you."

Parsons also noted that perhaps there were plenty of other actresses who weren't being offered roles outside their type, "half-expressed troupers."

Trevor and husband Bren followed up the chaotic days of the filming and promotion of *Borderline* with a summer holiday aboard their sloop, Pursuit, "If I make a single move, the boat will move with me. The picture has been fun but tiring and all I want to do is take it easy, fish and sail."

She loved sailing and her husband said, "When she goes to sea, she is no land-lubber. She knows all the nautical terms, their meanings and how to say them. Not every sailor's wife can do that. Claire could captain any trip if the need arose. However, she seems content to remain one of the crew. She doesn't even get seasick."

She had been banished from the boat pre-shooting as she had to stay out of the sun. If she spent even an afternoon outside, the tan she quickly acquired meant scenes in the film didn't match.

After the brief vacation she was soon back scanning every script that came her way, "I was looking for a good love story, but they're hard to find. For some reason they don't seem to be writing them anymore, yet the appeal of romance has never lost its appeal with the public. Speaking for myself, I would rather see and read a love story than any other type of entertainment or fiction."

Husband and wife were hoping to be able to find another project to work on together.

Trevor and Bren took pains to show themselves as an average American couple. Still she confessed whenever they encountered anyone outside the film industry she found herself working overtime to correct false impressions about Hollywood in general and herself in particular. Bren, who admitted he sometimes felt, "Good and mad about it," added "I tell them I'm proud of my work and proud of the place in which I live. I explain that both Claire and I are well-mannered because we're reasonably intelligent and well-educated people. We both speak several languages, like good music and the ballet and are patrons of the arts. Claire does a little painting and writing in addition to acting.

"We both contribute both time and money to every worthwhile charity which calls upon us.

"Our children lead normal, healthy lives and attend public schools."

After failing to find another property to work on together, *Best of the Badmen* (1951) was Trevor's next picture for RKO. The screen play was written by Robert Hardy Andrews and John Twist and it was directed by William D Russell and starred Robert Ryan, Jack Beutel, Robert Preston and Walter Brennan.

Ryan and Trevor were cast as persecuted fugitives in a color western and it is the outlaws of the Clanton and Younger gangs that are the heroes of this fictionalized biography.

After the Civil War, Union Major Clanton captures survivors of Quantrill's Raiders, and gets them clemency at the cost of shooting a mob member. Convicted of murder by a kangaroo court, Clanton escapes and joins the former raiders in a gang devoted to robbing everything protected by the corrupt detective agency of his enemy Fowler; culminating in a personal showdown.

During filming a flash flood had stranded members of the cast including Robert Ryan, Walter Brennan and Trevor in the Utah Mountains and many miles from their headquarters.

The LA Examiner reviewed the picture in June 1951 calling it another chapter of the violent Quantrill Raiders saga, "What makes this yarn interesting is that the outlaws aren't the only villains of the piece. Nearly everyone is heavy.

"There is no lack of action in this marathon chase...and the Technicolor picture exhibits a great deal of handsome scenery.

"A very impressive cast quite competently handle the acting."

In Universal's Casting Survey of 1956, which listed the contracts, availability, and amounts Hollywood's female actresses worked for, Claire Trevor can be found well down the ranks, behind Lauren Bacall at $100,000 per picture plus script approval, Joan Crawford at $200,000 and script approval, Greer Garson ($125,000), Deborah Kerr ($150,000), Maureen O'Hara ($80,000) and Barbara Stanwyck ($75,000). Trevor was available for just $30,000. She was not under contract and no further demands or possible difficulties are mentioned in the survey. Some actresses asked for percentages of net profits, or other stipulations. Perhaps because she was known to be a fine actress, cheap and easy to get along with, she continued to find herself with plenty of offers.

In 1951 she starred as Millie Farley in RKO's *Hard, Fast and Beautiful* which was directed by Ida Lupino, "Ida Lupino was a very good director, very warm, very sensitive, a very intelligent lady." Lupino herself made a cameo appearance, applauding at a tennis match in sunglasses. Trevor and Lupino had great rapport, "She was completely supportive of a woman and her needs as an actress. She was very intuitive." Trevor felt she was softer than a lot of men but said, "She wasn't wishy washy at all."

Lupino was already seen as a feminist cult figure; she had cut a path through the brush of the male dominated Hollywood establishment, but the thematic narratives of her films essentially led her to a dead end.

Lupino and Collier Young were producing three pictures for RKO, but Trevor was the first star the team ever signed. Until then they had worked exclusively with newcomers.

In *Hard, Fast and Beautiful* Lupino's melodrama leans heavily to the tragic. Casting both daughter and mother as tragic heroines, the film confronts the contradictions of being a woman in World War Two American society. Lupino exposes tensions through the conflict between mother and daughter, exploring class distinctions, irreconcilability of female passivity with aggressive social mobility.

Gordon (Robert Clarke) meets Florence (Sally Forrest), who shares his interest in tennis. But Florence has a supremely ambitious mother, Trevor, who intends to push her ahead and her tennis career rapidly advances, thanks to Trevor's manipulation and a promotion-minded coach; building toward the inevitable conflict.

Produced at a cost of $300,000 by Collier Young, husband of Lupino, the screenplay was by Martha Wilkerson from a novel by John R Tunis. Director of photography was Archie Stout.

Unlike most of the era's melodramas which attempt to resolve these conflicts with the forced 'happy ending', Lupino refused to consolidate the contradictions into a neat bundle and the movie ended with a defeated Trevor staring aimlessly at wind-tossed trash. No solution is offered. The sense of frustration often felt by women in the post war America is all too clear and made for uncomfortable viewing.

Amongst varied reviews was Variety's (5.30.51) ; "A low-budget film but its values stack up against more expensive productions. Claire Trevor socks over her character as the selfish mother. Tight editing and excellent photography."

Hoodlum Empire (Republic) was produced and directed by Joseph Kane in 1952. Trevor starred alongside Brian Donlevy, Forrest Tucker and John Russell in a fictional working of the innermost secrets of the overlords of the underworld by the Hearst paper's own Bob Considine, of the Kefauver Senate crime investigations, with Trevor the underworld siren patterned after Virginia Hill.

The problem of corruption and the "hoodlum empires" was seen as a most important issue in early 1950s America. People believed the gangsters were running the country without any challenge by the law.

The LA Examiner felt that the job done by Kane in exposing the issues in this movie deserved a special accolade and that it pulled no punches. Ruth Waterbury wrote, "I've been hearing about Joe Kane for some time now and Papa Yates has given him a strong cast to work with here.

"That wonderful actress, Claire Trevor, is just as commanding as she was in *Key Largo*.

"The very solid entertainment is all here – backed with something so much more important, a warning and a lesson to us all. *Hoodlum Empire* becomes a film of stature and integrity."

By and large however the picture was largely ignored and within months Trevor was back at work for MGM.

My Man and I (1952) was directed by William Wellman and starred Ricardo Montalban and Shelley Winters.

Montalban plays a migrant Mexican worker in California who is proud of his new US citizenship. Unusually Trevor is cast as a sour farmer's wife who makes a play for him.

"William Wellman directed me in *My Man and I* (1952) and *The High and The Mighty* (1954). He was a tough man – too tough. Ricardo Montalban was in *My Man and I*, he was the sweetest man. His wife was rushed to hospital to give birth. He asked Wellman if he could leave but Wellman wouldn't let him go."

He'd become something of a nemesis and Wellman and Trevor had had a big fight on the set of *My Man and I*. Later she said, "He could be rough. And I didn't really think the picture was very good. The book had had real suspense and excitement and it was lost in the picture. I don't know how or why. It was too long and they lost it. That was the whole meaning of the picture, the suspense. It should have been cut. Also they shot a whole sequence showing my past and how I met this man who became my whole life. I was the backstreet girl. They shot all that in San Francisco and then never used any of it in the picture. So when I turn up in the picture you don't know who I am. That destroyed me."

The movie was double-billed along with *The Devil Makes Three* also from MGM and, as everyone knew, when two pictures get thrown in for the price of one, neither was going to be a diamond. However, Ruth Waterbury, writing again for The LA Examiner, said that in fact they formed a good dramatic contrast, "And one thing they both have in common : each of them is superbly acted."

My Man and I, by virtue of cast, director and running time, was meant to be the more important. But movie goers preferred *The Devil Makes Three*, which starred Gene Kelly as an

Air Force captain and was largely shot on location in Germany. Not a good end game for Trevor.

In the same year she worked on *Stop, You're Killing Me* for Warner Bros. Directed by Roy Del Ruth from a play by Damon Runyon and starring Broderick Crawford, this was a direct remake of *A Slight Case of Murder* the stage play from 1938.

Stop, You're Killing Me was an updated version in color and with songs also thrown in for good measure. Critics of the new movie felt the songs added nothing, were light and exploitative and were not well presented. The drama comedy starred Crawford as an ex-beer baron trying to go straight after the repeal of the Volstead Act (the prohibition laws) and Trevor as his moll wife, Nora, just trying to make it and welcome in an air of respectability.

Original cast lists show Edward G Robinson as the star with the part of Nora uncast. Hal Wallis seemed to be generally unhappy with all the screen tests done, "They don't seem to get over what we're trying to get. This is a newly rich family who had been travelling with gangsters all their lives and now they are in the dough. Nora is trying to put on an acquired polish." Wallis hadn't tested Trevor up to then. He had seen tests of Ruth Donnelley and felt she wasn't in a big enough league for the picture, "I don't like Marjorie Rambeau either, she plays it too straight. And I don't want Lillard Parker in the part. None of these people seem to give anything. Nothing looked good about them. Let's line up a new batch of people."

Jack Warner personally sought out Shelly Winters and Lucille Ball, who were both unavailable and finally arrived at Claire Trevor who asked $50,000 but eventually signed for $25,000 for eight weeks.

Wallis was having more than casting problems and still had no script four weeks from the starting date. He wrote to the producer "I would occasionally like to get a complete script two to three weeks in advance of the starting date, so that I could have time to work on it properly."

Certainly both Broderick and Trevor were well placed to make gangsters and molls come to life for a new, post-prohibition generation. And Trevor's role was viewed favorably.

By 1953 Trevor went back to Columbia, this time to film *The Stranger Wore a Gun* directed by Andre DeToth and produced by Randolph Scott. DeToth particularly enjoyed working with Trevor and later commented, "Claire Trevor is a Barbara Stanwyck Junior…very similar in their approach to life and their approach to pictures."

Once again she found herself cast as a long-suffering, girl who knows her way around. Randolph Scott played yet another former Quantrill spy now in the Confederate army in an early 3D wide screen vehicle, which was shot for thrills and chills.

The critics of the movie were unsure about the 3D experiment with the LA Examiner complaining, "This Technicolor Western opus has a discomfiting way of throwing the action directly at you from the screen.

"Third dimension scenery and color filming will give you the urge to go visit the mountains whether you are a western fan or not. As for Randolph Scott, either you are a fan or not, for he always plays the same role. He now seems to be showing a bit of wear and tear and they are very smart to cast him with a maturely beautiful star like Claire Trevor so he doesn't appear ridiculous in his love scenes.

"Claire of course is a favorite, largely because she is such a good actress. Pretty hard to make a flop of a film she's in."

Marie Mesmer wrote in LA Daily News, "Ever had a horse sit on your lap? Well they practically do in *The Stranger Wore a Gun*." She enjoyed the action and the chase for gold through deserts and mountains.

However the LA Times writer felt the movie was ordinary, even in 3D, "This film gets the works, but even so fails to emerge as one of the better westerns."

At the end of 1953 she made her television debut in a half hour drama for NBC's Ford Theatre entitled *Alias Nora Hale*. Trevor discovered she enjoyed working in television, saying, "I can do in it what I can't do in pictures – play sympathetic normal roles. If a part has enough facets, I don't mind playing the bad girl. Bette Davis played one designing woman after another for years – but they were such marvelously interesting people. I'm tapering off in pictures. I think three or four TV shows a year are enough too. As for a TV series, never! Life's too short and frankly I'm not terribly ambitious."

She may have considered winding down but in 1954 another major opportunity presented itself with John Wayne's air-disaster picture, *The High and the Mighty*, a no-expenses spared project directed by her arch enemy, William Wellman. Produced by Wayne Fellows, the movie was adapted from the best-selling book by Ernest K Gann who also produced the screenplay and it was distributed by Warner Bros.

The High and the Mighty found her once again, the cheery loose-lady. Even though she was happily re-teamed with Duke she still failed to be won over by William Wellman, calling him, "Brusque, egotistical, not sensitive at all."

On the whole her sentiments were reciprocated and Trevor had not been the first name on Wellman's casting list and he rudely commented later, "I asked Joan Crawford, Ida Lupino, Barbara Stanwyck, Ginger Rogers, and Dorothy McGuire. Two of those I had helped in the past too. They all turned me down. Some were even insulted when I offered them the roles."

Many Hollywood stars accepted parts according to the number of lines they would have in the picture; how prominently they were going to emerge. But every role in *The High and the Mighty* was small and some newcomers had much bigger parts than even Wayne himself who said, "I guess they didn't think the roles were good enough for them."

Eventually Wellman was forced to concede, "To hell with the big stars. They think they know so much. I decided I could do without them by getting fine actors and actresses instead." When he eventually hired Trevor he was forced to retract earlier statements, relented and called her "One of the greatest, if not the greatest." Of course whilst they didn't like each other he still had to get a performance out of her and offered the occasional backhanded compliment. She was never taken in by him and didn't particularly working on the unusual movie.

Wellman and Wayne had acquired a new four inch lens which effectively brought all the actors in the plane close together. It meant shooting couldn't be cut often and so all the actors had to stay in place and in character for long periods of time. Despite the movie ending up a huge hit Trevor herself felt working on the "terrible picture" had been shudderingly tedious, "There were all those wide shots down the aircraft, so you just had to sit for hours doing nothing in case your left ear was supposed to be in the frame.

"Phil Harris was losing his mind; he didn't know what to do with himself. He was making his first dramatic picture and he hated it. We were all called every day. We all had to be there all day, every day, and maybe you'd not say a line. I brought a Scrabble board and taught Phil how to play. I'll never forget how cute he was. A darling man.

"Anyway, Bill and I got on better on this picture. He was an old style director and he was good at building enthusiasm," Trevor later commented, very much tongue-in-cheek.

She was again nominated for an Oscar as best supporting actress, "But I thought my part was ruined when the preamble to my character was cut out during the editing."

Dorothy Manners reviewed the movie in LA Examiner, "Wayne turns in the finest performance of his life, playing with magnificent restraint. No attempt is made here to mention the performances in order of excellence because all are wonderful…particularly Claire Trevor as another blonde with a shaky future."

The Hollywood Reporter considered Claire Trevor to be "the perfect actress."

This movie also saw Trevor attending some of the most glamorous red-carpet premiers of her career and she found herself attending star-laden performances, all over the country alongside old friend Wayne who this time was one of Hollywood's leading lights.

The High and The Mighty gave her something of a boost and the following year she made yet another major film. *Man Without a Star* was a United Artists project directed by King Vidor and starring Kirk Douglas and Jeanne Crain.

In 1954 she had signed with Universal to renew her friendship with Douglas as Idonee, who was yet another in the production line of hard-boiled saloon keepers with a heart of gold.

She received $10,000 for one week's work and was billed as 'third co-star'. At least it paid to play the bad movie character and her name was still to the forefront of every casting director's mind when a good, bad girl was required.

As in earlier Press Releases she found herself saying, "It's ironic, but audiences seem to like bad girls because they have more character than good girls." It all sounded a bit old hat by then.

During production the set had been full of atmosphere that Trevor put down to the magnetic presence of Douglas who had spent time ensuring he had perfected techniques in riding, roping and shooting with wrangler-stuntman, Fred Carson.

Unlike most actors, Douglas didn't retreat to his changing room after he had finished shooting, but stayed on set, working with Vidor and the rest of the cast. He said he wanted to create something different and Trevor enjoyed working with him; she considered him to be a professional in every sense.

Whilst Douglas was credited with his 'ridn'along, singin' a song' performance, the picture flopped and went largely unrecognized with scarcely a mention for either Crain or Trevor despite Bantam Books and Universal launching a paperback edition of Dee Linford's *Man Without a Star* to help promotion.

The Hollywood Reporter called the film, eighty percent entertainment and twenty percent plot.

New York Times called it "Not the greatest to emerge from Hollywood Manufacturers." "Claire Trevor, who has been through this sort of thing before, does right well by the role of the lady of easy virtue."

NY Daily Mirror, "Claire Trevor steals the femme honors in one of the better westerns."

Joan Crawford fought for Trevor to be cast alongside her in *Johnny Guitar* (1954), jealous of the much younger Mercedes McCambridge, who was eventually cast, and Trevor failed to get an opportunity to work with the legendary actress, instead going on to star in *Lucy Gallant* for Paramount, a picture directed by Robert Parrish.

She worked alongside Jane Wyman, Charlton Heston and Thelma Ritter in a fashion salon tale set in a booming oil town in Texas. Wyman has to choose between handsome husband, (Heston) or establishing the most fabulous department store in Texas.

LA Examiner felt it was an unusually good show, sumptuously produced, "Claire Trevor is broadly amusing as a social snob who once was much less good than she should have been. Personally, I'd like to see this wonderful actress given the opportunity to play a refined human being, for a change."

Trevor herself said, "Hollywood stars aren't weighing the importance of parts these days. They're weighing the importance of the picture. Studios are turning out more important pictures now than ever in the history of the business. It's common for a production to cost two and three million dollars. Cost isn't essential. What counts is getting a good picture. A substantial role in any of these important productions is much better for an established player than the lead in a mediocre picture."

Trevor believed a new approach to the selection of roles was taking place amongst Hollywood's most sought after personalities. "Playing the title role of Lucy Gallant affords Jane the outstanding assignment of her career, I was offered the second starring feminine role and snapped at the chance.

"It was to be one of Paramount's most important VistaVision productions of the year, adapted from a story in Good

Housekeeping and screenplayed by John Lee Mahin and Winston Miller, two of the best writers in the business. Lucy Gallant had all the ingredients to make an outstanding picture."

Trevor believed that appearing in such productions brought a star before massive audiences, "Today's hits are seen by millions more fans. Hollywood never realized it could reach such vast audiences with a single picture. A performance in a top film attraction is viewed by five times more people than used to see the average movie.

"I don't care how long my part lasts on screen. Just let it mean something when I'm there."

Film producers of course were largely being forced into creating better product, threatened as they were by the arrival of some top class television entertainment.

But Trevor didn't feel her next role in *The Mountain* (Paramount) 1956, contributed very much to anything. It would also be her only film appearance of the year. *The Mountain* was directed by Edward Dmytryk and Trevor starred opposite Spencer Tracy and Robert Wagner. Spencer and Wagner played an unlikely pair of mountain climbing brothers.

Years later Trevor left no doubt in anybody's mind about her attitude to the picture, calling it, "Horrible. Oh God that was a terrible picture! It goes on and on forever. Robert Wagner looked twelve years old and Spence had already got heavy and old-looking. It was ludicrous."

The picture was shot on location in Chamonix in the French Alps. Trevor's role as a quiet villager, in love with Tracy was mercifully brief.

"Don't ask me why, but Hollywood script writers still don't seem to write women. They convey certain traits and characteristics, but in the overall character conception they seldom penetrate inside to reveal 'whys and wherefores that the woman is like she is. Only occasionally have I come across what I call a "whole woman" in my film career. What I mean by this is a completely motivated female, with all the emotional subtleties and by-play that is woman. It's my opinion that I've been playing 'half a woman' most of these years, because of the sketchiness of the writing. Accordingly, some of the women I've portrayed have been tough to make interesting.

"Playwrites have a far greater success in depicting women. I remember a gratifying experience at LaJolla last summer playing the love-starved spinster in Arthur Laurents' *The Time of the Cuckoo* a role later re-created by Katharine Hepburn on screen.

"It's the male era in motion pictures and scripters write for the Gables, Tracys, Douglases and Lancasters, but they pass over us girls. We are in for the ride, in most cases, providing the romantic or the heavy story interest. But we don't have the values in our roles that are given to the men. It's very discouraging.

"Every time I pick up a script, I say to myself, 'well maybe this is it!' let me say that in television I also managed to find a perfect woman as Fran in the production of *Dodsworth* that I did with Frederick March and Geraldine Fitzgerald.

"I found some satisfaction in the role of the mountain woman, Marie in *The Mountain*. She is a comfortable person and you can find her type as we did when we encountered the villagers of Chamonix. I wish feminine roles of stature would come along as they do for men. Writers should be gentlemen and remember us girls. We'd like a break."

She may have disliked the picture but LA Examiner critic, Dorothy Manners called it "spinetingling."

Trevor recognized that her movie career was slowing. She considered that it was unlikely that any more big breaks were likely to come her way. She refused to be down-hearted and instead of pining she determinedly increased her radio, television and stage appearances, often appearing as a guest artist. Unlike many movie stars she embraced the advent of live television, and as her film career declined, she simply accepted more and more supporting roles through the period.

"I enjoyed working in television where I could do what I can't in pictures – play sympathetic, normal roles.

"I did a lot of television drama in the fifties. That was an experience to be doing an hour and a half live on television. It was terrifying but very exciting."

She remained busy and sought after and won an Emmy in 1956 for Best Live Television Performance for an Actress as Fran, the flighty wife of Fredric March in *Dodsworth* on NBC's Producer's Showcase. "That was my favorite performance of any I ever did. That's the one time I'm almost proud of what I did. To me, that was such a beautiful play. There, I played a real woman. We rehearsed it for two weeks and it turned out great. I remember we were standing on set during the countdown ready to start … and the perspiration was just pouring off me I was so nervous."

She said it was frightening because a hand would suddenly grab her off the scene, throw her into a change of clothes and throw her back on into the next set.

1956 saw Trevor earning approximately $30,000 for *The Mountain* compared to the $125,000 that Jean Simmons was taking and Lauren Bacall's $100,000 per picture. She may have been earning less per movie, but she remained in high demand and always had something lined up. She very rarely rested and looked to each next step enthusiastically.

She replaced Bette Davis in *If You Knew Elizabeth* on Playhouse 90 in 1957, "I don't know why she didn't do it, but that was another terrifying thing. Gary Merrill was looking for this character and he'd go to her friends and her parents and each one remembered her in a different way, so it was like playing six different characters. It was interesting and exciting.

At the same time she was working on the stage and starred on Broadway in *The Big Two* which was directed by Robert Montgomery. She also did summer stock in Laguna in the play, *The Time of the Cuckoo*. Years later she said, "I was sorry I ever did it. The stage is not for me anymore."

She briefly turned her attention back to the film world and in 1958 starred in *Marjorie Morningstar* for Warner Bros. Directed by Irving Rapper and produced by Milton Sperling, from the best-selling book by Herman Wouk, the picture co-starred nineteen year old Natalie Wood and Gene Kelly. It was shot on location at the Scaroon Manor resort in the Adirondacks and New York's Central Park.

Trevor had not made a film the previous year but quickly found herself enjoying the work again. The movie had been in pre-production for over two years after Jack Warner purchased the rights to the book. During this time Wouk served in a supervisory capacity and the selection of the cast. The search for Marjorie was a coast to coast affair. Sperling estimated that he tested over three hundred candidates. Elizabeth Taylor had been one of the stars hoping to win the part of Marjorie, but MGM refused to loan her out.

Sperling said, "My feeling about the girls, based on the film I saw today, is negative. Sandra Rehn photographs well in color, and Phyllis Newman has sparkle in her performance, but on the whole they didn't show themselves to good advantage. On the part of Rose, which eventually went to Trevor, he wrote,

"Incidentally, the woman who played the mother did not help any. I got one big positive confirmation from seeing these tests ... the mother will not have a Jewish accent in the picture!"

Trevor didn't stay on location but commuted from her new home in Balboa. She later commented, "I enjoyed working with the younger stars like Natalie Wood who was a dream girl. I loved her like my daughter. And the affection was returned, with Wood saying, "I wanted to play Marjorie more than any role in the world. Usually when a person wishes for a thing so wholeheartedly, the fulfillment comes as an anti-climax. This was not the case with Marjorie. As I got into the picture and worked with such talented persons as Gene Kelly and Claire Trevor my enthusiasm grew."

While working as a counselor at a summer camp, college-student Marjorie Morgenstern falls for 32-year-old Noel Airman, a would-be dramatist working at a nearby summer theater. Like Marjorie, he is an upper-middle-class New York Jew who has fallen away from his roots, and Marjorie's parents object among other things to his lack of a suitable profession, such as medicine or law. Noel himself warns Marjorie repeatedly that she's much too naive and conventional for him, but they nonetheless fall in love. As they pursue an on-again-off-again relationship, Marjorie completes her studies at Hunter College, and works to establish an acting career, while Noel first leaves the theater for a job with an advertising agency, but later completes a musical he'd started writing before he and Marjorie first met. Meanwhile, their relationship deepens and they plan to marry, but after the musical's critical failure on Broadway, Noel runs away. Marjorie finally tracks him down at the summer theater where they first met, and, realizing that this is probably where he belongs, finally gives up on the relationship.

Wood was frequently visited on set by Robert Wagner, who she later married. All the stars of this movie found themselves under close scrutiny at the resort which was full of guests who enjoyed seeing what film stars do when they are not filming.

The LA Examiner wrote, "No two people could have been found more perfect for the roles of Natalie's parents than Claire Trevor and Everett Sloane. Bewildered and confused by the course of unhappy events, by the deviation of their daughter's allegiance to family faith, and yet standing by to aid and help, Miss Trevor and Sloane in gestures and words are plain wonderful."

Her next movie was *I Stole A Million* 1959, directed by Frank Tuttle and produced by Burt Kelly and co-starring George Raft. It wasn't a major success and Trevor took stock of her career at this watershed period. She was reinventing her career at a time when the roles on offer were beginning to change and following her success as the mother opposite Wood, and in 1959 she became the matronly type as Ma Baker in an episode of *The Untouchables*.

Hollywood Means a Long Time Ago To Me

By the advent of the sixties her career choices had begun to dwindle further and the days of glamour were largely behind her. There were fewer film offers and those that came her way were for the matronly type. In *Two Weeks In Another Town* (MGM) 1962, directed by Vincente Minnelli and shot in Rome, Trevor again starred with Kirk Douglas and Edward G Robinson.

After spending three years in an asylum, washed-up actor Jack Andreus (Douglas) views a minor assignment from his old director Maurice Kruger (Robinson) as a chance for personal and professional redemption. He has been offered two weeks of dubbing work by Kruger who is also close to the end of a fading career. Both men are hard pressed, especially by Kruger's shrewish wife, Clara (Trevor). The movie saw Trevor portraying one of the nastiest characters in her rogue's gallery.

On December 20th, 1962 she played the new Head Nurse at Blair Hospital in an episode of *Doctor Kildare* called The Bed I've Made.

She continued to receive more television work than she could ever accept. She and Bren were living in Newport Beach and she took up painting saying, "Painting is a lot cheaper than going to a psychiatrist." She was always busy and seemingly happy with her lot and happy to work on whatever came her way that she could fit into her breakneck schedule.

In 1963 she starred as a well-meaning mother in 20th Century Fox's *The Stripper*, produced by Jerry Wald from the play by William Inge, *A Loss of Roses*. The picture was directed by Franklin Schaffner and co-starred Joanne Woodward and Richard Beymer. Trevor was contracted at $50,000 for ten weeks.

She played a small town widow, Helen, whose son, Kenny, shows an interest in an older performer in a girlie show. The mother in the original play didn't have a clearly defined role and the relationship between mother and son wasn't sympathetic, but the screenwriters decided to focus more attention on them and to sweeten the role of the mother. Kenny seeks out floosies because a nice girl would ruin his relationship with his mother.

When Wald was in pre-production he wrote, "We must try and decide what the playwright was trying to say and whether we can say it better. A rough guess behind the decline of many of the motion pictures of recent years I am sure is because too many of the characters have left audiences with a feeling of indifference or distaste. All of us know that a good film demands an emotional investment on the part of the audience. They must care deeply about the people they are looking at. They want these characters to be human and, being human, subjected to all the frailties and human strengths, but in too many films in too many instances audiences feel they have been associating with pasteboards."

When he began his search for the mother, he was looking for someone who could be sweet, cuddly, adoring and with a degree of breeding and some strength of character. The role was viewed as a key element of the film and the producers along with writer Inge considered Lee Remick and Jennifer Jones as well as Trevor. As Wald had said, he wanted someone human and who the audience could feel affection for, "If this sounds like a call for the return to heroic characters on the screen I would say that it probably wouldn't be a bad idea."

"Unusual plots are a dime a dozen; interesting characters on the screen, real people, are rare and represent the highest expression of the writer's art."

When the role was offered to her Trevor viewed it as one of the more normal ones and she appreciated it. On her acceptance,

Wald wrote to her, "I want you to know how delighted I am that you have chosen to play Helen Baird. I feel that you will bring to this role a unique balance of warmth and humor. On this first day of shooting, may I extend to you my gratitude and heartfelt good wishes."

Wald continued extending Trevor's part in the movie and several times contacted the script writers with suggestions; "Build Helen's reaction to Kenny's and Lila's relationship – her awareness of what's going on, her sensitivity to the possibility that something might erupt between them." He wanted as much warmth and emotion out of the character of Helen as possible and he warned his writers, "She must never emerge as a cold woman. At all times the audience must care about her problems, understand her desire to make something out of Kenny. We certainly don't want her to emerge as a clingy mother, or a dominating one. She should have the ring of truth about her."

Wald must have been a dream-come-true for Trevor who had been lamenting the poorly written female roles for so long. Here was a producer pushing for her character development. He saw Helen as in her mid-forties who works during the day as a nurse. She is a tired looking woman who long ago gave up her youth and no longer strives to make herself sexually attractive. There is still beauty though in her sad face, a face that has looked on tragedy and never forgotten it.

"If this picture has emotional wallop, one which will hit the audience in the head as well as the heart, we can't keep from having a big hit. It has to be so human that it is interesting to men and women of all types and classes."

As the filming progressed Wald continued to send memos to Trevor praising her performance. "Helen Baird is coming to life on the screen. You are doing a simply wonderful job and I want to express my admiration and thanks. I also appreciate the script suggestions you have made, which have been most helpful and perceptive."

He also wrote to the director congratulating him on eliciting "wonderful performances" from Trevor.

Whilst Trevor won no accolades for her performance the movie was Oscar nominated for best costume design.

The following two years saw Trevor concentrating more on her painting and sailing but in 1965 she was back working on *How To Murder Your Wife* (UA). Directed by Richard Quine, she co-starred alongside Jack Lemmon, Virna Lisi, Terry Thomas and Eddie Mayehoff. Trevor played the domineering wife of Mayehoff in producer-writer George Axelrod's comedy.

There gap between movies increased and it wasn't until 1967 that she starred in *The Capetown Affair* (20th Century Fox) about South African secret agents attempting to save confidential microfilm before it falls into the hands of Communists.

Directed by Robert D Webb, this movie starred James Brolin and Jacqueline Bissett in a re-make of Samuel Fuller's *Pickup on South Street* (1953). Trevor had the Thelma Ritter role as a bag woman mixed up with the communist ring.

Although this was her last movie appearance for nearly twenty years she continued picking up further important television roles and was seen in episodes of Ford Theatre, GE Theatre, Playhouse, Desilu Playhouse, *The Untouchables, Dr Kildare, Alfred Hitchcock Presents, The Love Boat* and *Murder She Wrote*.

In 1968 she returned to the stage after a prolonged fourteen year absence, playing the cigar smoking lesbian in *The Killing of Sister George*.

"I mostly stopped working after the sixties. There are no scripts being written for older women so you don't get the parts. I didn't continue on like Bette Davis and Barbara Stanwyck. The only time I would have worked was if something irresistible had been offered me. Bette Davis had nothing in her life except her career. I had many other interests and a happy marriage and she didn't have that.

"When I worked on *Murder She Wrote* with Angela Lansbury it was just like the early movies to me. First of all they said, 'you're going to stay in a hotel right near the studio' and I said, 'Great. I can roll out of bed and get to the studio in nothing flat.' Well we never shot anything in the studio. Everything was on location so they said, 'Your call will be for five in the morning. We'll pick you up from the lobby of the hotel.' Five in the morning! I'd been retired for some time when I made that and got up when I felt like it, this was a jolt. So we'd stay on location all day and not get back to the hotel till nine at night.

"It was very rugged. I said, 'never again.' But I enjoyed working with Angela.

"A TV series is something I couldn't do. I was way out of training. Angela was in the routine but it wasn't easy for her either. She's amazing. On Wednesday she goes home and Thursday morning she starts a whole new episode with a new director, new script, new clothes. I mean it's just unbelievable.

"Looking back on Hollywood, I think the demise of the studio system is just too bad because they knew how to make stars. They weren't business men like they are today. To be the head of a big corporation doesn't mean you know anything about show business. They were showmen in those days and they were marvelous."

She was unlike most actors from Hollywood's Golden Age in her view of the old studio system and she said it had been her time as a contract performer that had made her what she was, "You had to do a lot of work that you didn't want to do; that's true – a lot of crummy pictures, but they knew how to build a star and they knew what to do with you. They also taught you everything."

Trevor had always been a willing learner and the contract system also offered her some stability during difficult economic times. She tended to look back on her career at this time through rose-tinted glasses, because it had never been an easy ride for her and she hadn't always enjoyed it, but she now often found herself criticizing new productions and she felt modern film-makers tended to take lazy options and that many modern films made up for their shortcomings by having too much violence thrown in.

"I have great respect for the technicians of those days too. It breaks my heart when I see films have been colorized, because the whole mood is lost. Each cameraman took great pride in black and white effects and getting the mood right, people lit scenes carefully. Kit took hours and hours to get lighting right and Karl Freund, the cameraman on *Key Largo*, took forever."

Although she was largely retired, in 1976 she co-starred with Rock Hudson and Leif Ericson in a twenty one week national tour of *John Brown's Body*, a narrative poem adapted for the stage by Charles Laughton.

Then in the late 1970s twin tragedies struck and Trevor's life changed again forever. In 1978 she lost Charles, her son from her marriage to Cylos William Dunsmoore, in a plane crash over San Diego. Then, in 1979, her husband, Milton Bren died of a brain tumor. "This was something I never got over. I felt completely alone."

During Bren's illness she rarely left his side as he underwent a series of surgeries.

She and Bren had lived in Newport Beach for twenty five years and they had spent months on end sailing their trawler, The Lady Claire, together. Bren had won the first Newport to Ensenada International Yacht Race.

He had also helped develop Sunset Strip, "Milton had a hobby that turned into a fortune. He built office buildings on Sunset Boulevard." After his death Trevor sold the buildings to David Geffen.

Trevor was almost destroyed by the tragedy, but to help cope with the loss, she moved back to New York where she attempted to build a new life, surrounding herself with old friends. "Newport Beach without Milton is unendurable so I have pulled up stakes completely."

The fortune Bren had established enabled her to lease an unfurnished luxury apartment boasting four bedrooms and three bathrooms. She confessed, "I think they are the best proportioned rooms in New York. Initially she had hesitated to take on such a large establishment, until her stepson, real estate developer, Donald Bren told her, "You'll get used to it, it's better to have more space than too little."

She lived in a suite at the Hotel Pierre through the early 1990s and had a friend, Ann Downey, help to design what was then one of the most spacious apartments in the city.

She never became reclusive and she made many new friends, including Claudette Colbert and Rock Hudson. Although she and Hudson never worked together they had become close friends during their sailing days. In New York he lived just across

Central Park, although he continued to maintain a home in Beverly Hills.

Heartbroken but indomitable, Trevor remained active and traveled all over the country and commented in an interview for Architectural Digest in 1992, "I'm eighty three and I don't care who knows it."

She also continued painting, but admitted, "I don't know how good the paintings are, nor do I care. I'm filling my hours with pleasure, and you can't take that away."

In 1982, aged seventy three, she made her farewell starring film role as Sally Field's acid-tongued mother, Charlotte Banning, in *Kiss Me Goodbye* (20th Century Fox). Directed by Robert Mulligan the picture had a cast including James Caan, Jeff Bridges and Mildred Natwick.

The film marked a long awaited return to Hollywood and also to the studio where she started her illustrious career for her first film in fifteen years. She commented, "Hollywood means a long time ago to me."

She said she accepted the role in *Kiss Me Goodbye* because she got to be funny in it. "I said 'yes' because I got to be glamorous in Arnold Scaasi gowns." She loved working with Sally Field who she came to adore. "In fact the whole cast was really terrific.

"The film is reminiscent of pictures made in the golden era of Hollywood when there was light, sophisticated comedy. It has a feeling of the original *Topper*, with Cary Grant and Constance Bennett, which my husband produced by the way. Those charming comedies, with a combination of fantasy, love story and real amusement. I think *Kiss Me Goodbye* has the best of them all."

She was however disappointed in the reviews, "It was only meant for entertainment. The critics killed the picture. Why did they take axes and slaughter it? I really don't understand. I thought it was a darling picture."

In fact the movie was considered by critics to be an unfunny remake of the Brazilian hit *Dona Flor and Her Two Husbands* (1978).

In August 1985 Trevor jetted from New York to be at her friend, Rock Hudson's bedside, but she later confessed that she wasn't even sure if he recognized her.

In August 1987 co-workers, Lawrence Tierney and Harry Lewis were amongst guests paying tribute to Trevor at the American Cinema Awards Foundation's 'An Evening For Claire Trevor.' The film clips used at the Tribute included *Key Largo, Stagecoach,* and *Two Weeks in Another Town;* selected as reminders of her enduring range, versatility and her quiet professionalism. She herself chose for the full-length feature presentation the 1941 Western, *Texas* in which she co-starred alongside, William Holden and Glenn Ford, saying she picked it for the scenery and because it was fun to make. Once again her role in it was small, but it emphasized her reputation as a modest woman full of appealing talent that seemed to come easily to her. The audience that night included Joseph Cotton and Glenn Ford.

As she took to the stage she said simply that she never looked back although admitted that the evening had given her a sense of her accomplishment and that the retrospective had highlighted an odd thing, in that when she was handed her first film contracts it had been because producers liked the way she handled stage comedy and yet she had rarely been offered comedy roles throughout her long and illustrious career.

Looking back on her career she said, "Most of the films I did were just daily work and I didn't really get excited about anything except something like *Stagecoach*. When you work with a director of that magnitude you're in heaven. By the same token I enjoyed *Dead End* but that was a day and a half.

She appeared in the made-for-television picture *Breaking Home Ties* in 1987 before returning to live in Newport Beach and retiring fully from the big screen saying, "I had worked like a demon and I knew it was a job. Saturday night, you never could plan on going out to dinner because we'd only break for an hour and then be back working until the early hours of the morning."

Claire Trevor's story is ultimately one of success obtained through hard work, her determination and drive to make good, and an unusually relaxed attitude toward the film industry, the individuals who inhabited it alongside her and her adoring fans.

As her career came to its close she admitted, "Acting wasn't the main impetus of my life. Working to me started from necessity. I never based my whole life and dreams on a career. I had many other things. I had many friends, a wonderful family and a marvelously happy marriage. But when I worked I gave it everything I had because that's the way I do everything."

She continued to enjoy painting and said, "To me acting and painting are closely related. You need imagination for both. I don't know how good my paintings are, nor do I care. I'm filling my hours with pleasure and you can't take that away."

She had loved painting all her life and said, "Golf never appealed to me. It's just a diversion. I didn't think I had much to offer but I found it cheered me up when I've been in despair. It's always there when you want it.

"I've got a houseful of paintings. I never knew if they were any good, but Milton always said they were great. He faithfully framed each one and put it on the wall. The beauty of painting is that you don't have to be a genius. You can get the same feeling of satisfaction and yet be mediocre. No one can take it away from you. Of course, it's better if it turns out that you have talent. I hope someday to find out that I have, but if it's not to be, it won't be the end of my world. It fills my hours with pleasure."

She also maintained her committed active stage interest and association with The School of Arts at University of California in Irvine. She and her husband had donated $10 million to further its development for the visual and performing arts which included three endowed professorships.

Clark Andrews, who Trevor divorced in 1942, died in Los Angeles in 1985.

In 1994 she moved back to a spacious new home in Newport Beach where she launched a new social life. Now in her eighties she appeared to have an inexhaustible vitality although no apparent interest in returning to acting.

Like many other older Hollywood stars she did lament modern film making saying, "I don't like all the violence and nudity," However she also accepted there were occasional exceptions citing *Dead Poet's Society* which she had enjoyed.

By now Trevor was essentially retired and she spent her time painting, traveling and enjoying her family and friends.

In 1998 she made a guest appearance at 70th Academy Awards as part of a tribute segment called, Oscar's Family Album. Michael Caine refered to her as "living legend"

Looking back on her career in an interview in Films in Review in 1983 Trevor had said, "I was stupid in a lot of ways.

Promotion. I hated it with a passion, because after every picture, you'd have to pose for fashion stills. And you'd spend the whole day in the still department changing clothes and holding poses. And you know, when you're a young girl, that's such a bore. Loretta Young and I made a picture together, *Second Honeymoon*, and she was a perfect movie star. She did everything right. She'd comb her hair and then she wouldn't move. Marvelous. And one day they said to both of us, 'All right ladies, you're finished.' It was about one o'clock. I said, 'Wow' off came the false eyelashes. Know what she did? She called the still department and said, 'I have the afternoon off. Let's make some stills.' That's how she was. If you're going to be a movie star, be a movie star…

"What I really didn't do all the years I had a chance to, was work with the publicity department along those lines. I should have devoted more time to it but I would skirt them and try to get out of everything they set up for me. I hated that part of the business which was stupid because if you're in a public business you should cater to it and I didn't – not nearly enough.

"I was much more interested in acting. I really didn't pay attention to the other side of the business. Even though I got some really poor scripts I always tried to do my best."

She was unassuming about her career but reserved her highest accolades for those she worked with, particularly Ford and Huston.

Her career however was hugely significant in Hollywood history. The little blonde from New York was a top class actress who managed to incarnate the history of her country and its women on film. She may not always have had the best roles but she always seemed to get one great line that carried a punch and caught the attention.

"Do what I tell you and you'll always go wrong." Lily (*Best of the Badmen*)

"Where did you get your luck Valerie? Or does God pity the wicked?" Marion (*The Velvet Touch*)

"You shouldn't kiss a girl when you're wearing a gun. It leaves a bruise." Velma (*Murder, My Sweet*).

With apparent ease she had been the quintessential hard-bitten floozy with the heart of gold and her on-screen persona was typified by her portrayals of nearly every conceivable type of bad-girl, from hooker to gun moll. She had been inexplicably relegated to mostly supporting roles, primarily in B movies. But the husky voice that delivered the classic quotes possessed a talent that could not be denied and, more than any other actress, she represented the classic film noire in seven pictures of the era, *Street of Chance* (1942), *Murder, My Sweet* (1944), *Johnny Angel* (1945), *Crack-Up* (1946), *Born To Kill* (1947), *Raw Deal* (1948), and *Key Largo* (1948).

On January 14th 1999 Trevor gave back to the craft she loved by donating a further $500,000 to UC Irvine to finish restoring the thirty year old Village Theatre where over a hundred plays, dances and concerts are performed each year by the university's acclaimed drama, music and dance departments. Trevor's gift was made to fund a series of improvements including a glass lobby.

"The theatre is a great place to expand one's horizons and learn about people and what makes them tick. UCI has a wonderful drama department which gives young adults – before they face the hardships of reality – a chance to soar with their imaginations. I am thrilled to be able to help them achieve such goals and, perhaps, to be a small part of their dreams."

Apart from her gift to the university she had also been involved with The Orange County Arthritis Foundation, although she preferred to keep a low profile and refused to sit on boards.

"I made mostly B pictures. I never had a Howard Hawks fighting for me, or a Von Sternberg like Dietrich had. Or a Mauritz Stiller, like Garbo had. And then it became just work. I am talking about making movies in eighteen days. I am talking about working Saturday nights. I am talking about doing three pictures at once.

"Darryle Zanuck really didn't know what the heck to do with me. I wasn't his type. The big stars on the 20th Century Fox lot were Alice Faye, Betty Grable, really sort of glamorous women or beautiful singers and dancers. I just didn't get anywhere with him."

Recalling the 20th Century Fox of days gone by, Trevor said, "It was huge. It encompassed all of Century City and ran from Beverly High to Pico Boulevard. Olympic boulevard was just a dirt road. In those days the studio had its own dress designers and they were terrific. Of course, I'd be asked to pose for publicity stills in the twenty five to thirty gowns from each picture. It was a very busy, active and exciting place to be."

"Cut; Print"

On 8th April 2000 Trevor died in hospital near her Newport Beach home from an undisclosed respiratory illness.

The funeral service was private.

She had made over sixty films in a fifty year career

Step son Donald Bren said of her passing, "Claire was a special woman whose lifelong passion was to bring joy to others. Her legacy will be the many ways she touched people. She was a great lady."

Trevor had maintained a keen interest in stage work after her retirement and had become associated with The School of Arts at the University of California, Irvine, which renamed the school theatre, The Claire Trevor School of the Arts posthumously. Her Oscar for *Key Largo* and her Emmy for *Dodsworth* are proudly displayed behind glass at the school's Arts Plaza complex.

Trevor had enjoyed life to the full. She liked to dance, laugh, swim and play tennis. When she was in bed she didn't like getting up and when she was up she didn't like going to bed. She was contented doing whatever she was doing, wherever she was. The friends she made along the way, she kept till the end, constantly enlarging her group. She devoted herself to them and her family. Ultimately, they took precedence in her life over her career. They kept her sane in her insane world and negated any sense of regret she may have felt when things didn't turn out the way she had hoped.

She had explained before her death, "I learned my craft. I worked hard – like a demon actually, because I worked so much. I was paid nicely. But let's face it, the parts I would have given my soul for – real women, real parts – Bette Davis got."

She also understood that she hadn't become a top star because she didn't possess the drive that energized the likes of Davis, "I didn't know that to make a real career in Hollywood you had to become a personality, had to cultivate publicity departments and become known as 'The Ear' or 'The Toe'.

"So many actresses I knew lived for the profession alone. Their personal lives were secondary. They neglected their children, their husbands. But you can't live that way without losing. Those girls ended up losing everything. Joan Crawford ended up without friends, family, anything. Bette Davis the same way. There were many like that.

"I don't think female movie stars have particularly happy lives, I rather doubt that even Katharine Hepburn had a happy life. But I'm sure about myself. I had a happy life; ninety percent of my thoughts were not directed to career."

Trevor rarely reflected on her performances but she remained amazed at the fan mail she continued to receive, "With television running the old movies, I get mail from around the world. They say things you don't expect the modern audience to say – that 'whatever role you've done, you've brought such truth and believability to it, and dignity, charm and expertise'. Well, most of my performances I did came from my own feelings, my own heart. I never thought those lousy pictures would give anyone pleasure…yet they have."

In 1995 Trevor had refused to write an autobiography arguing it would have taken her the rest of her life although it would have been a wonderful story, "But I hate looking back."

Claire Trevor had been an elegant and eloquent example of Hollywood stardom and the best of her movies stand vivid testament to her talent. She had remained consistently unassuming and generous, reserving her highest accolades for those she called the masters, directors Wyler, Ford and Huston. But for all her modesty her career was immensely significant in cinema history and labeling her as a B movie actress or a queen of film noire seems to be dismissive of that talent. Claire Trevor was, without any doubt, a superlative actress who embodied the development and conflicts of her country and its women on film with dignity.

The smokey-voiced performer; once described as sounding like delicious trouble, had regularly breathed life into a variety of rather dull affairs. She had been known as the Queen of the B's, low budget action movies that rounded off double bills. But when she got a chance at an A picture she had always given it her best shot. She was modest and the rarest of actresses who was so good, her talent appearing so effortless, that viewers and producers alike often took her for granted. Film buffs cherished her, as did the very best directors.

In 2001 she made a posthumous appearance at the 73rd Academy Awards, honored in a segment of those who had passed away that year

For her contribution to the motion picture industry, Claire Trevor has a star on the Hollywood Walk of Fame at 6933 Hollywood Blvd.

In 2010 the Blu Ray edition of Stagecoach was released.

Quotes

Using one's imagination to the fullest is necessary for a happy life

Don't fall in love with your leading men. Of course that's just what I did

I don't know why they call it Hollywood anymore. The whole meaning of the town has changed. Hollywood has lost an enormous amount of quality.

What a holler would ensue if people had to pay the minister as much to marry them as they have to pay a lawyer to get them a divorce.

Key Largo... I could have stayed on that picture for the rest of my life. I adored it.

The studios knew how to build a star, and they knew what to do with you. They also taught you everything.

The only thing I knew how to do then was act, and at that point I didn't even know much about that.

References

Killer Tomatoes: Fifteen Tough Film Dames Hagen, Ray; Laura Wagner (2004) McFarland.

Many of the quotes used in this volume come from an interview Trevor gave in 1992 for the publication *At the Center of the Frame: leading ladies of the twenties and thirties* by William M. Drew, published by Vestal Press, 1999.

Femme Noir Bad Girls of film   Karen Burroughs Hannsberry McFarland (1998)

Is That Who I Think It Is? Vol 2   Patrick Agan
Ace Books (1975)

Broads   Ian and Elisabeth Cameron. Movie Paperbacks series, published by Studio Vista (1969)

Warner Bros Archives

Universal Collection

LA Examiner Review clippings

Edward Small Collection (USC Cinema – Television Library.)

Jack L Warner Collection (USC Cinema – Television Library)

King Vidor Collection (USC Cinema – Television Library)

Jerry Wald Collection (USC Cinema – Television Library)

Films and Filming (January 1990)

Classic Images (December 1989)

Films in Review (1963 and 1983)

Picturegoer (1948 and 1949)

Silver Screen (1939)

Film Weekly (1938)

British Film Institute archives.

Archives and special collections * of the Margaret Herrick Library at the Academy of Motion Picture Arts and Sciences.

*See below

-Hedda Hopper Collection.

-Marty Weiser Collection (Poster Art from Warner Bros, a series of pencil sketches of cast of Key Largo).The collection consists of production files, correspondence (both personal and professional), subject files, photographs, pressbooks, and clippings. The production files contain publicity-related material, including advertising budgets, clippings, correspondence, and press releases for hundreds of films, primarily Warner Bros. releases. The subject files contain publicity material on film personalities.

-Fox Films

-Paramount Press Sheets

Ronald Davis Oral History Collection on the Performing Arts, Degolyer Library, Southern Methodist University, Dallas.

Architectural Digest April 1992 "Claire Trevor: A Spacious New York Apartment for Key Largo's Best Supporting Actress"
      SML Aronson

Awards

1938 Academy Award Best Actress in a Supporting Role nomination for *Dead End*

1949 Academy Award Best Actress in a Supporting Role winner for *Key Largo*

1955 Academy Award Best Actress in a Supporting Role nomination for *The High and The Mighty*

1955 Emmy nomination for Best Actress in a Single Performance for: Lux Video Theatre (1950) episode 'Ladies in Retirement'

1957 Emmy Award Best Single Performance by an actress winner for Producer's Showcase : *Dodsworth* (1954)

1965 Golden Laurel nomination for Supporting Performance, Female for: How to Murder Your Wife (1965) 5th place.

1995 Golden Boot

Star on the Walk of Fame (year unknown) Motion Picture
At 6933 Hollywood Blvd.

Filmography

1. Breaking Home Ties (1987) (TV)　　Grace Porter
2. Murder She Wrote (1987) (TV)　　Judith Harlan
3. The Love Boat (1983) (TV)　　Nancy Fairshield
4. Kiss Me Goodbye (1982)　　Charlotte
5. The Cape Town Affair (1967)　　Sam Williams
6. How to Murder Your Wife (1965)　　Edna
7. Woman of Summer (1963)　　Helen Baird
   aka The Stripper - USA *(original title)*
8. Dr. Kildare (1962) (TV)　　Veronica Johnson
9. Two Weeks in Another Town (1962) Clara Kruger
   aka 2 Weeks in Another Town - USA *(poster title)*
10. The Investigators (1961) (TV)　　Kitty Harper
11. Alfred Hitchcock Presents (1961)　　Mrs Meade
12. Alfred Hitchcock Presents (1956)　　Mary Prescott
13. The United States Steel Hour (1960) (TV)
    aka The U.S. Steel Hour - USA *(alternative title)*
    - The Revolt of Judge Lloyd
14. The Untouchables (1959) (TV)　　Ma Barker
15. Wagon Train (1959)　　C.L. Harding
16. Westinghouse Desilu Playhouse　　Savannah Brown
    (1episode, 1959)
17. Marjorie Morningstar (1958)　　Rose Morgenstern
18. Playhouse 90 (1957) (TV)　　Elizabeth Owen
19. The Mountain (1956)　　Marie
20. G.E. True Theater　　Cora Leslie (2
    episodes, 1954-1956)
    aka General Electric Theater - USA *(original title)*
    aka G.E. Theater - USA *(informal short title)*
21. Producers' Showcase (1956)　　Fran Dodsworth

22. Schlitz Playhouse (1956)   Mary Hunter... aka
    Schlitz Playhouse of Stars - USA *(original title)*
    aka Herald Playhouse - USA *(syndication title)*
    aka The Playhouse - USA *(syndication title)*
23. Climax! (1956)
    aka Climax Mystery Theater - USA *(alternative title)*
    - The Prowler (1956) TV episode
24. Lucy Gallant (1955)   Lady MacBeth
    aka Oil Town - USA *(reissue title)*
25. Stage 7 (1955) (TV)
26. Lux Video Theatre (2 episodes, 1954-1955)
    aka Summer Video Theatre - USA *(summer title)*
    - No Sad Songs for Me (1955) TV episode
    - Ladies in Retirement (1954) TV episode
27. Man Without a Star (1955)   Idonee
28. The Ford Television Theatre   Felicia Crandell
    (2episodes, 1953-1954)
    aka Ford Theatre - USA *(short title)*
    - The Summer Memory (1954) TV episode Felicia Crandell
    - Alias Nora Hale (1953) TV episode
29. The High and the Mighty (1954)   May Holst
    aka William A. Wellman's The High and the Mighty - USA*(complete title)*
30. The Stranger Wore a Gun (1953)   Josie Sullivan
31. Stop, You're Killing Me (1952)   Nora Marko
32. My Man and I (1952)   Mrs Ansel Ames
33. Hoodlum Empire (1952)   Connie Williams
34. Best of the Badmen (1951)   Lily Fowler
35. Hard, Fast and Beautiful (1951)   Millie Farley
    aka Mother of a Champion - USA *(alternative title)*
36. Borderline (1950)   Madeleine Haley

37.	The Lucky Stiff (1949)	Marguerite Seaton
38.	The Babe Ruth Story (1948)	Claire Ruth
39.	Key Largo (1948)	Gaye Dawn
40.	The Velvet Touch (1948)	Marian Webster
41.	Raw Deal (1948)	Pat Cameron
42.	Lady of Deceit (1947)	Helen Brent
	aka Born to Kill - USA *(original title)*	
43.	Bachelor Girls (1946)	Cynthia
	aka The Bachelor's Daughters - USA *(original title)*	
44.	Crack-Up (1946)	Terry Cordell
45.	Johnny Angel (1945)	Lilah 'Lily' Gustafson
46.	Farewell My Lovely (1944)	Mrs. Helen Grayle
	aka Velma Valento	
	aka Murder, My Sweet - USA *(original title)*	
47.	The Woman of the Town (1943)	Dora Hand
48.	Good Luck, Mr. Yates (1943)	Ruth Jones
49.	The Desperadoes (1943)	Countess Maletta
50.	Street of Chance (1942)	Ruth Dillon
51.	Crossroads (1942)	Michelle Allaine
52.	The Adventures of Martin Eden (1942)	Connie Dawson
	aka High Seas - USA *(reissue title)*	
53.	Texas (1941)	'Mike' King
54.	Honky Tonk (1941)	'Gold Dust' Nelson
55.	Dark Command (1940)	Miss Mary McCloud
56.	The First Rebel (1939)	Janie MacDougall
	aka Allegheny Uprising - USA *(original title)*	
57.	I Stole a Million (1939)	Laura Benson
58.	Stagecoach (1939)	Dallas
59.	Five of a Kind (1938)	Christine Nelson
60.	Valley of the Giants (1938)	Lee Roberts
61.	The Amazing Dr. Clitterhouse (1938)	Jo Keller
62.	Walking Down Broadway (1938)	Joan Bradley

63.	Big Town Girl (1937)	Fay Loring
64.	Second Honeymoon (1937)	Marcia
65.	Dead End (1937)	Francey
	aka Dead End: Cradle of Crime - USA *(reissue title)*	
66.	One Mile from Heaven (1937)	Lucy 'Tex' Warren
67.	King of Gamblers (1937)	Dixie Moore
68.	Time Out for Romance (1937)	Barbara Blanchard
69.	Career Woman (1936)	Carroll Aiken
70.	Fifteen Maiden Lane (1936)	Jane Martin
71.	Star for a Night (1936)	Nina Lind
72.	To Mary - with Love (1936)	Kitty Brant
73.	Human Cargo (1936)	Bonnie Brewster
74.	Song and Dance Man (1936)	Julia Carroll
75.	My Marriage (1936)	Carol Barton
76.	Navy Wife (1935)	Vicky Blake
77.	Dante's Inferno (1935)	Betty McWade
78.	Spring Tonic (1935)	Bertha 'Betty' Ingals
79.	Black Sheep (1935)	Jeanette Foster
80.	Elinor Norton (1934)	Elinor Norton
81.	Baby Take a Bow (1934)	Kay Ellison
82.	Wild Gold (1934)	Jerry Jordan
83.	Hold That Girl (1934)	Tonie Bellamy
	aka 'Hold That Girl!' - USA *(promotional title)*	
84.	Jimmy and Sally (1933)	Sally Johnson
85.	The Mad Game (1933)	Jane Lee
86.	The Last Trail (1933)	Patricia Carter
87.	Life in the Raw (1933)	Judy Halloway

Soundtrack:

1. Key Largo (1948) (performer: Moanin' Low (uncredited))
2. Crossroads (1942) (performer: 'Til You Return (uncredited))

Self:

1. The 70th Annual Academy Awards (1998) (TV) Past Winner
2. Victor Borge Birthday Gala (1990)
3. The Hollywood Greats John Wayne (1984) TV episode Hollywood Greats - USA *(new title)*
4. An All-Star Tribute to John Wayne (1976) (TV)
5. Hollywood and the Stars (acknowledgment) The Man Called Bogart - (1963) TV
6. Person to Person (1961) (TV)
7. The 29th Annual Academy Awards (1957) (TV) Presenter: Cinematography Awards
8. The 28th Annual Academy Awards (1956) (TV) Co-Presenter: Scientific & Technical Awards
9. The 27th Annual Academy Awards (1955) (TV) Nominee: Best Actress in a Supporting Role & Presenter: Best Writing, Motion Picture Story
10. A Star Is Born World Premiere (1954) (TV)
11. The 25th Annual Academy Awards (1953) (TV) Presenter: Best Sound
12. Picture People No. 3: Hobbies of the Stars (1941)
13. Picture People No. 2: Hollywood Sports (1941)
14. Screen Snapshots Series 19, No. 5: Art and Artists (1940)
15. Screen Snapshots Series 18, No. 10 (1939)
16. Screen Snapshots Series 16, No. 10 (1937)
17. Sunkist Stars at Palm Springs (1936)

Archive Footage:

1. 1939: Hollywood's Greatest Year (2009) (TV) Interviewee
2. You Must Remember This: The Warner Bros. Story (2008) Interviewee
3. Biography - The Barrymores (2004) TV episode Gaye Dawn
4. The 73rd Annual Academy Awards (2001) (TV) Herself (Memorial Tribute)
5. Off the Menu: The Last Days of Chasen's (1997) (uncredited) Herself (with Jane Wyman)

The Claire Trevor Album

Claire Trevor and Clark
Andrews enjoyed playing
tennis

Trevor's first home, purchased ready furnished, during the war.

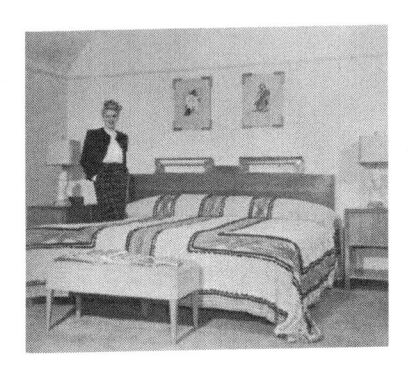

Advertising paid off handsomely

164

1938

WHAT ACTION PICTURE!
WALTER WANGER presents
STAGECOACH
Directed by JOHN FORD
WITH
Claire John
TREVOR · WAYNE
A JOHN FORD Production
ANDY DEVINE · JOHN CARRADINE
THOMAS MITCHELL · LOUISE PLATT
GEORGE BANCROFT · TIM HOLT
Released thru UNITED ARTISTS

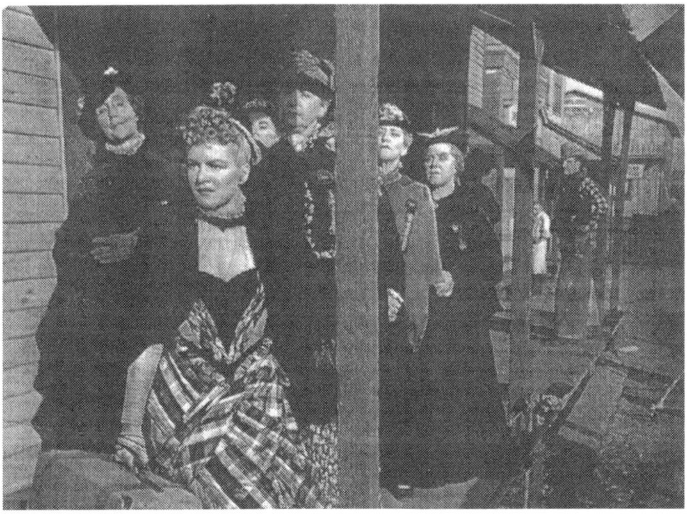

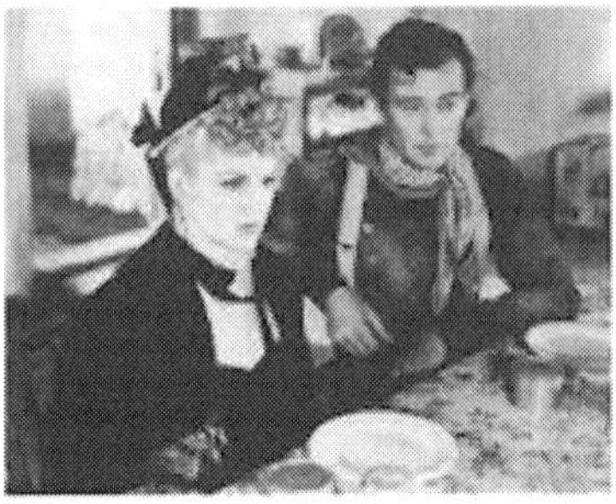

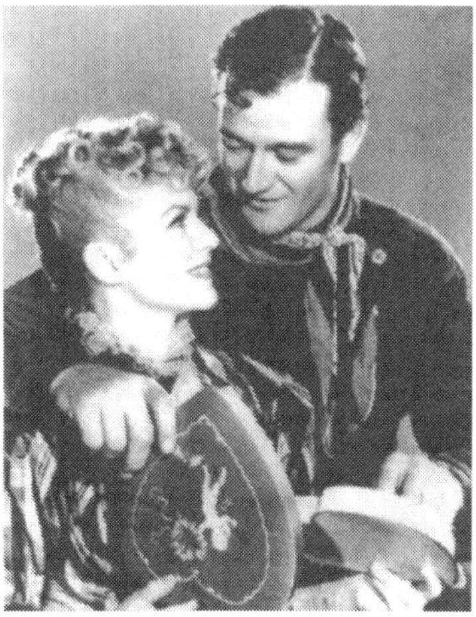

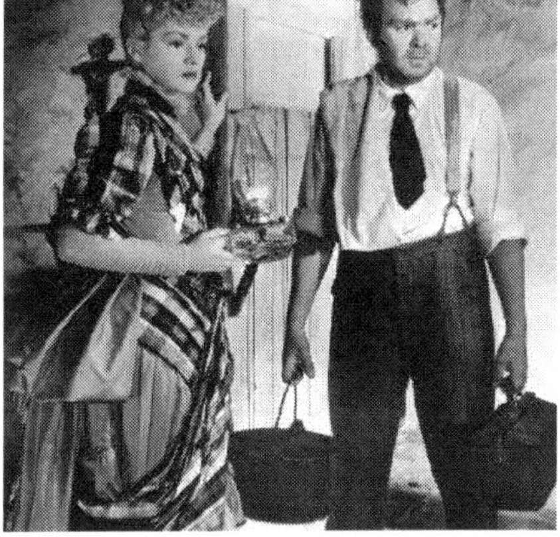

Wayne and Trevor teamed in *Stagecoach, The First Rebel* and *Dark Command*

169

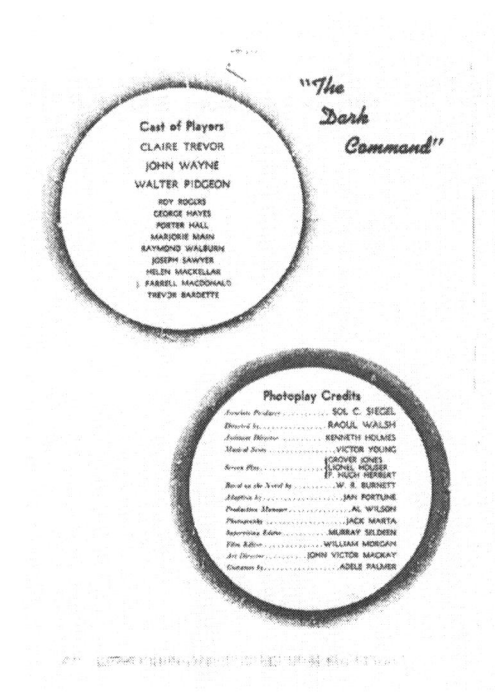

HOW TO MAKE FRIENDS AND INFLUENCE MILLIONAIRES
Andrew Stone
presents
GAIL RUSSELL · CLAIRE TREVOR
ANN DVORAK · ADOLPHE MENJOU
Mink coats...
yachts...diamonds...
see how they get
husbands who can
buy them.
"The BACHELOR'S DAUGHTERS"
EUGENE
LIST
with
Jane Wyatt · Billie Burke
Produced and Directed by ANDREW STONE

With Dick Powell in
Murder, My Sweet

Film Noir

1948

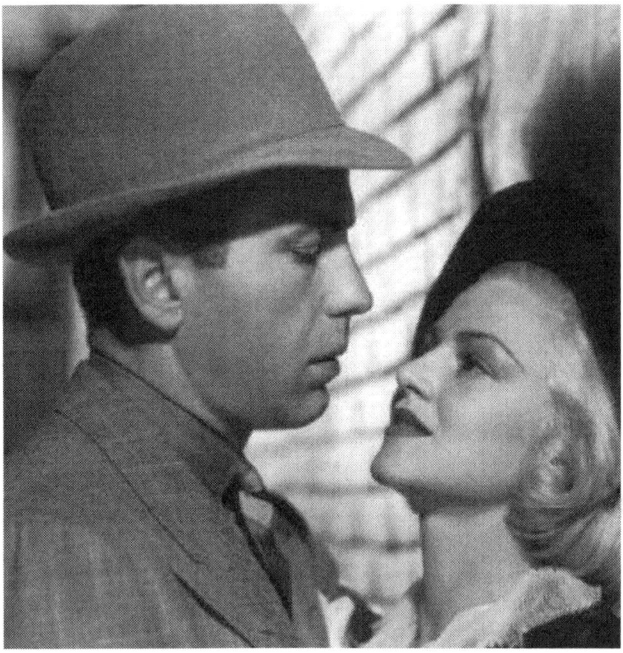

Bogart, Bacall,
Robinson and Trevor

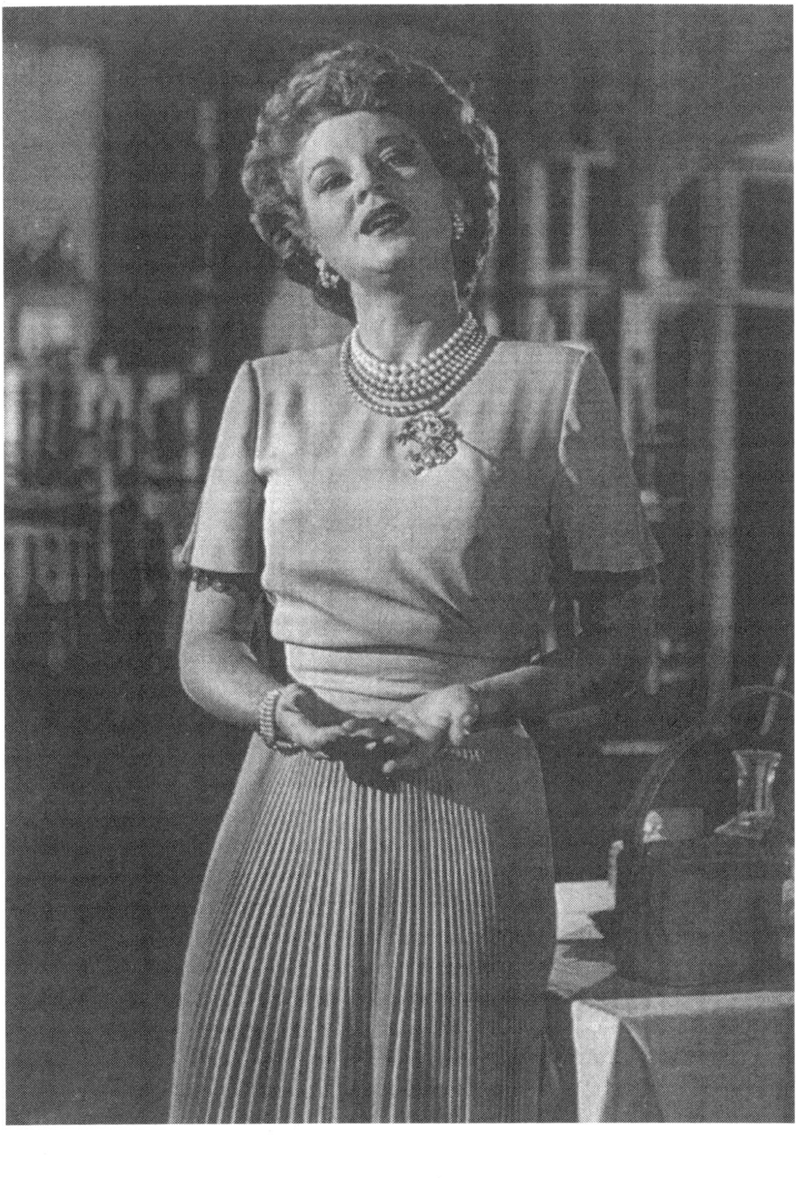

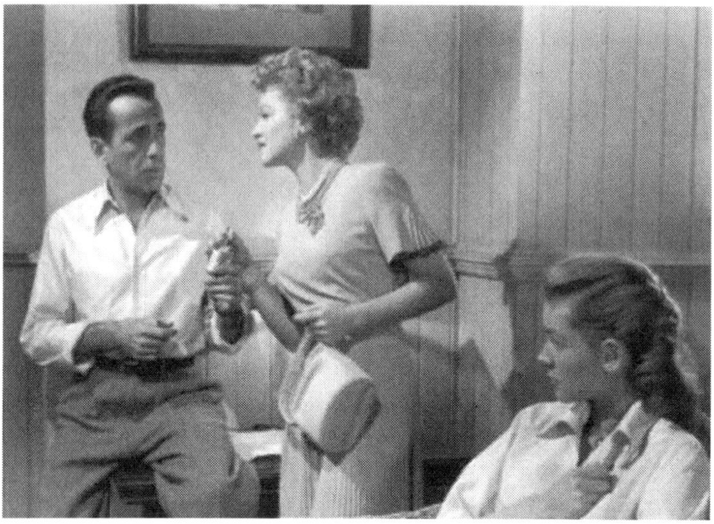

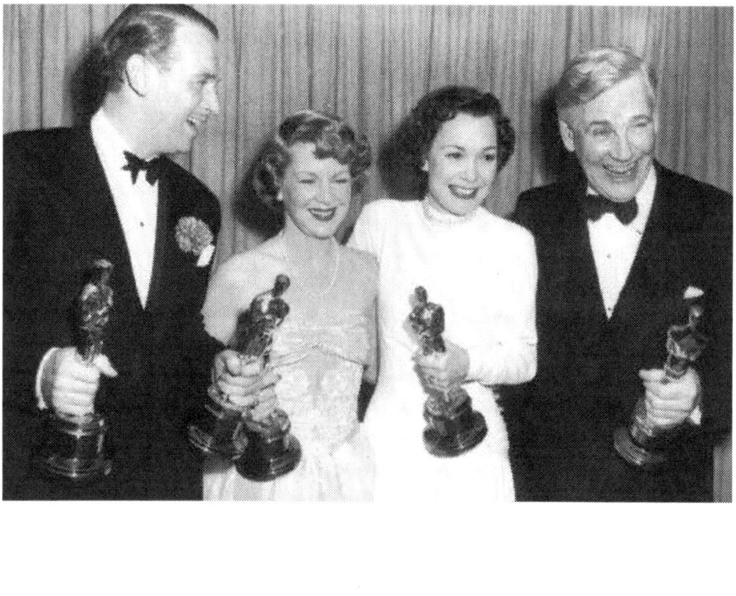

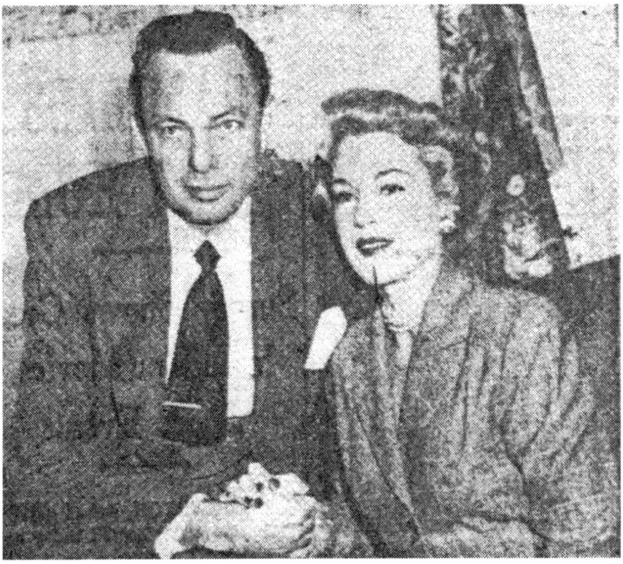

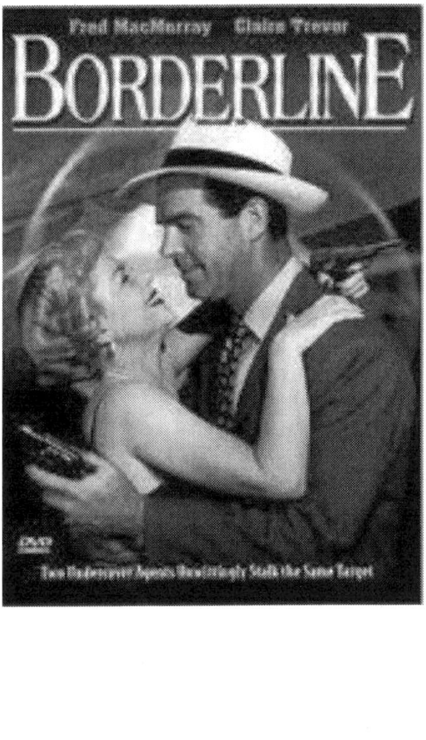
Fred MacMurray
Claire Trevor
BORDERLINE
DVD

THEY MET LIKE THIS

THEY LOVED LIKE THIS

AND THIS

WAS THEIR WEDDING NIGHT!

A Federal Agent..(he sez)

A Lady Cop.. (she claims)

!!! and they're trying to
pinch each other in the
funniest places!

(..South of the Border)

FRED MACMURRAY
.. topping the laughs in
his "Egg and I" and
"Family Honeymoon"!

CLAIRE TREVOR
.. in her first performance
since winning the Academy
Award in "Key Largo"!

WHEN HE FOUND OUT SHE WAS A LADY COP ..

He took the law into his own hands!

He just loved the
way she "pinched"
him.. in fact he
pinched her back!

"J. EDGAR NEVER TOLD ME THERE'D
BE MOMENTS LIKE THIS..!

He's got
a babe on his hands,
a killer at his heels,
and a hot million bucks
in his pocket !

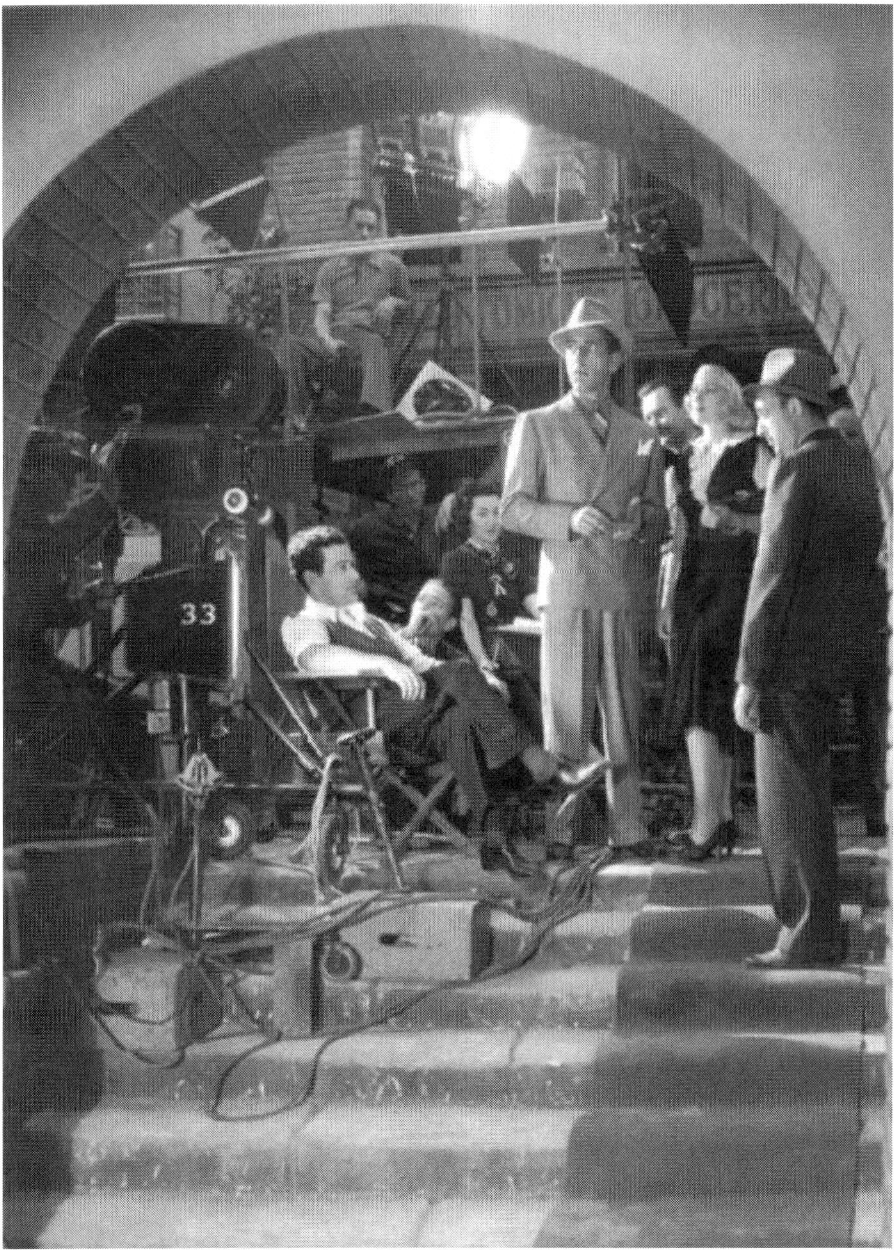
33

He hid his past
like the scars on his back
and he carried fear in his holster
and tonight he waited
to collect his share
in the strangest bargain
a man ever made with a woman!
KIRK DOUGLAS
JEANNE CRAIN
CLAIRE TREVOR
MAN WITHOUT A STAR
Technicolor
WILLIAM CAMPBELL
RICHARD BOONE
MARA CORDAY · MYRNA HANSEN
THEATRE

THE COLDEST
KILLER
A WOMAN
EVER LOVED
Lawrence Claire Walter
TIERNEY · TREVOR · SLEZAK
Born to Kill

With great friend
Rock Hudson

An Evening With
Claire Trevor

Also by C. McGivern

John Wayne; A Giant Shadow

The Lost Films of John Wayne

Ronald Reagan: The Hollywood Years

The Romy Schneider Story

Where Have All The Cowboys Gone?

And on the horizon

Edward Woodward: The Equalizer